GUILT, SHAME AND FEAR

THE CATALYST OF SPIRITUALITY

PAMELA WALKER

outskirts
press

This book is dedicated, first, to my Lord and Savior, Jesus Christ, for without Him, nothing is possible.

To my wonderful, tolerant, and understanding husband, Mr. Ronney Walker, Sr., who has stood by my side even when I did not deserve it. He has been my knight in shining armor from day one, even while I was the thorn in his side. Thank you, honey.

To my mom, who has been my inspiration, my confidant, and a perfect example of patience and understanding. To my son, Darryl Jones, whom I am so blessed to have—the best son ever whose struggles with mental health and addiction are not unlike my own, and we both know that God has the last word. To my grandchildren, Ke'shannah, Tondie, and Jay, who have given me a reason to become a better me. Finally, to my father, John B. Jones II, for showing me so much love, even without saying the words; rest peacefully, Dedda.

TABLE OF CONTENTS

PREFACE

CHANGE IS IMMINENT, whether it's good or bad, whether we like it or not. As much as we try our damnedest to stop it or at least control it, we cannot stop change from occurring, but more importantly, change is necessary. I am convinced through my own life experiences that those who make up our surroundings, including family, friends, coworkers, or even a stranger, have the potential to significantly alter who we are mentally, emotionally, and spiritually. However, the further I got into recounting some of my childhood memories for the purpose of this book, the more I realized that there may have been another reason for the consequential change in me, in addition to the human surroundings, that played a role in the manifestation of feelings of insecurity and unworthiness. I may have been born with the particularly challenging inability to stay focused that caused me to be insecure. I would often find myself focusing on other things while I was supposed to be learning in the classroom or having a general conversation with others. Is it possible the feelings I had of insecurity and low self-worth were misdirected? Is it possible that it was all in my head that the people in my circle, close friends or not-so-close friends and family, were to be blamed for the way I turned out? Maybe.

All that said, I do believe that most people we meet are quite inspiring in their own way as well as positive. The people we meet will inspire us to be kind, understanding, unselfish, and motivated. But what about the undercurrent? What about the dark side of these potentially valuable entities? The dark side, as my niece Sharmaine referred to it, sums up what I have gained from this group for the most part, or at least that is how I felt about it during my childhood and well into adulthood. I realize that some of us get bored with details that we believe are far removed from the real issues, but, at least in my case, the problems began in my childhood, far removed from the moment in my life when I realized the many emotional challenges I faced later in my life. It is always important to get to the root of any trauma, so bear with me through my childhood stories.

Growing up I was always nervous about being around more than one person at a time because I felt like the more people that were around me, the bigger the chance was that someone would notice that I was different. I didn't want them to tease me or talk about me amongst each other so I was always apprehensive about opening my mouth to join a conversation, knowing that I may say something that might have nothing to do with the conversation because I could not keep up with the conversation sometimes or I felt that my contribution didn't add anything of value to the conversation. I wanted to be a part of the group, but I didn't want to participate in the group, if that makes sense.

Here he comes again. Why does he keep making me do something I do not want to do? I don't want to do this.

Why don't they like me? I want to be friends with them. I want to be smart like the girls with pretty barrettes.

I hear the loud, angry voice coming from the room again. Then, knocking and banging as if someone was being hurt badly. There were only two people inside the room. I know who the victim is.

She was being beaten. The violence I hear makes me afraid for the victim. I want to comfort her, the little girl thought. She went into the room when he left and hugged the victim; she could see that the woman had been crying, but all she could do to comfort her was ask her, "Do you want me to get you some water?" The little girl told the victim she had a dream in which she had seen the abuser in a casket, but she lied. She had a conscious thought of him in a casket.

The little girl knew then that she would never provoke anyone to beat her. Little did she know that her life would take her down the very same violent road of physical abuse.

I began to realize that my feelings did not matter. People could hurt me. I did not trust them. I had experienced how mean they could be. I began to fear the humiliation and physical harm they could impose upon me, and because I feared being the victim of these things, it was impossible for me to fit in. I would stay in my corner unnoticed, wishing they liked me, but strangely I did not like them. I felt I was better than them because I would never treat others as I felt they treated me. I thought they were mean, and they thought I was crazy. Later in my life they thought I was nothing but a crackhead, they thought I was insignificant. As it turns out, so did I.

From the time I was about eleven or twelve, I was convinced that I should be afraid of what others thought about me because if they did not like me, I would be left out of the conversation. I would often notice that people gave each other a side glance as if to say, "What is she talking about?" I would get nervous among those I was not comfortable with or if the person who was speaking spoke too long, I may lose focus and respond incorrectly making my response sometimes confusing, sometimes it was humiliating. I blamed others for not being understanding and labeling me as crazy. This has been the case throughout my life but today I have learned that before I leave any conversation I am sure to question whether or not I had been understood, having notes helps me tremendously. I was convinced that I was not as good as everyone else. I was convinced that I was not pretty enough or smart enough to be a part of them without being ridiculed.

A quote from American poet, memoirist, and civil rights activist Maya Angelou comes to mind: "I've learned that people will forget what you said, people will forget what you did, but people will never forget how you made them feel."

It only took one family member to start the dimming of the sun and to take me into the dark side.

I turned to alcohol and drugs to help me feel good about myself and to be able to feel comfortable in my own skin. Ultimately, drugs and alcohol became my masters, effectuating another point of darkness for me. I was mocked, judged, and openly ridiculed by mostly women. I was beaten by men. I was comforted by none. All of this was initiated by one person—my uncle—and maintained by many. Anger, resentment, shame, guilt, and humiliation became significant components in my long battle with my fears.

As we go through life, we find ourselves searching for ways and things to manage or outright deny our fears. Drugs and alcohol were the things for me, denial came in the form of displaced emotions.

I had become so fearful of the humiliation and shame people could inflict upon me that I would shy away from defending myself from all the rude and mean comments that came my way. The fear got worse as the years went by. I experienced panic attacks whenever I was confronted by someone, even as far back as elementary school. It is difficult to act tough when you are afraid, but I did just that—I acted. On the flip side of the coin, it takes courage to react to any perceived danger in spite of fear. I realize now that God had blessed me with courage even back then.

Another prong in my story is the fact that "hurt people, hurt people." What about the shit I did to others? What about how I made them feel? You see, after so many years, even though I was hurting, it did not give me a pass to inflict the same shit on others. The thing I did constantly after I got clean from drugs and alcohol was "speak my mind" without understanding that I might have hurt someone's feelings—exactly the thing others did to me. It was understandable, but totally unacceptable. This cycle had to be broken.

Today, the sun shines as it ever has for me. But how did this happen? Pain was my motivator. I could not take the pain anymore. I needed to unpack all of what I know today as gifts. Yes, guilt, shame, and fear turned out to be my gifts. Spirituality was the key to finding God. Spiritual wounds, spiritual bankruptcies, and spiritual growth led me on a spiritual journey.

When I found God, I found peace. When I found God, I found hope. When I found God, I found myself.

My primary purpose in writing this book is to lead my readers to a different way of life—a life of spirituality. I am not religious. I still struggle from time to time with maintaining spirituality. The life I have today is the best I have ever lived because I have been able to find God in the midst of the struggles we all have in this thing we call life. At this very moment I had a revelation—the Lord has been with me throughout my whole life, and because He is with me, I can air my dirty laundry to complete strangers without shame, fear, or guilt. Yes, I am another you, I am flawed. Let the chips fall where they may. Praise be to God! This is my testimony.

FROM INNOCENCE
TO SHAME

IT ALWAYS AMAZES me when I hear folks recalling their childhood. Most seem to have happy memories. According to the 2014 article "What Is Your Earliest Childhood Memory?" in *Psych Central News* by Janice Wood, few adults remember anything that happened to them before the age of three. It also claims in a new study that it is about the age of seven when our earliest memories begin to fade.

The memories I have of my childhood are vague, at best. I do not remember playing with my brother and sisters before age six, possibly because my sisters were a few years younger than me and my brother was, well, my brother. There are no birthday parties that I can remember. I do not recall any fun times that have stuck in my memories, nor do I remember having any childhood friends prior to the age of about eight. I am not saying that there were not any good childhood memories, but the memories I do have are detailed memories of some of the worst parts of this time in my life. Why is that? The answer to that question is, for whatever reason, trauma has a lasting effect on us, and trauma has a way of negating anything good we may have experienced. That is my hypothesis.

This is what I do remember. As a matter of fact, I will never forget. I remember the apartment we lived in. I remember the bed I slept in. I remember my uncle and the smell of his breath. I remember feeling a certain way, but I did not know what the feeling was. I remember I was five.

My mom and dad left early in the mornings for work. My mom dropped my sisters off at the sitter in the mornings as well. I do not remember where my brother was, but I believe we all shared a bedroom; my mom and dad had the second bedroom. My uncle was also living there, but I do not remember where he slept. The bed I slept in was against the wall on the left side as you walked into the room. I remember a window at the foot of the bed. I remember being awakened, as I had been before, by my uncle. Again, he climbed into my bed. It was clear exactly what he wanted me to do. He guided my hands to his penis, encouraging me to hold it. I know I was facing him because I could smell his breath. It felt to me as if his "visits" lasted forever, but I can't be sure of that. To this day, from time to time, I can still smell his breath. I did not know what sex was then, but as the years went on, I associated the smell with sex. Remember, I was young, so the timing of the occurrences may be a little off, but the feelings I had were unmistakable. I also cannot help but wonder if my mother's brother had violated me prior to my memories of him doing so. I say this because when a child molester or rapist gets caught, more likely than not, it was not the first time this person committed such violations.

In elementary school, we would open school with the song "My Country, 'Tis of Thee" in an open area. There were no chairs; we all sat on the carpeted floor. The carpet was a bluish-gray color. I used to love that part of the morning, but something happened to me. I remember feeling different, as if I were not like all the other kids. I felt as if I might have done something wrong, but I was not sure what. I remember smelling my hands; I felt unclean. Today, I know what that little girl was feeling. It was shame.

My family moved out of our two-bedroom apartment around 1972 into our first single-family home. My uncle came too. This time, he stayed in the basement and my sisters, brother, and I had bedrooms on the top floor. He never came for a morning visit again. The memories of the incidents were removed, or perhaps I just blocked them out. However, my uncle was still attaching himself to me. He started to treat me as if I were his girlfriend of sorts. I was now about eight or nine. He would repeatedly ask me to grease his scalp or plait his hair. In order for me to do his hair, I would sit on the sofa while he sat on the floor between my legs. I just did not feel right, but I never told him no, and I do not know why—perhaps because he was an authoritative figure, or perhaps I was afraid of him.

My uncle died in 1976. He was twenty-two years old. He was killed by his father. A case of mistaken identity. Long before he left this earth, I was left with shame. I just did not fit in anymore. I was always on the outside looking in and hoping someone would see that I was a good person.

I never told my parents or anyone else what my uncle did to me. Think about it from a kid's perspective. I knew then that it was supposed to be a secret even though he did not say anything to the effect of "it's our secret." I was not sure if I should tell on myself if that makes sense. I was the one who did something nasty, and I was ashamed to say what I had done. I mean, I cannot be exactly sure why I did not tell my parents, but one thing is certain—I knew that I was not supposed to be holding my uncle James's penis while he did whatever he did to please himself.

My dad died in 2006 without knowing what my mother's brother had done to me. I told my mother about it around 2012. That was the year I got serious about my sobriety. I kept hearing my AA sponsors and speakers talk about their childhood, and that their childhood experiences were related to the battle of the disease of alcoholism, so I wanted to perhaps start a conversation with my mother about what my uncle J had done.

My mother's reaction was not what I'd expected, but I was not surprised by her reaction either. She expelled a small gasp and then, "What!" I could see that she was clearly hurt by what had happened to me. She never brought it up again. I did not go into any details with my mom because I knew it would hurt her even more. I was forty-two at the time so she could not help even if she'd wanted to. Let me just say that my wonderful mother has always been kind of subdued when it came to expressing or showing any emotions. Everybody has a story. I am almost 100% certain that her story, if told—a portion of it at least—would be like my own.

I cannot be one hundred percent certain that what my uncle did to me was the sole culprit of my introduction to shame, but what I can tell you is that I can absolutely remember, very vividly, the thoughts and feelings I had at the time, and the fact that what I say happened to me is real.

FROM SHAME TO HUMILIATION

I **HAVE NEVER** been diagnosed with Attention Deficit/Hyperactivity Disorder (ADHD), but I know enough about it today to conclude that I may have suffered with this disorder. When I look back to my years of school, starting in elementary school, I would often find myself unfocused and distracted. I tried my best, but eventually I would fall behind. In junior and senior high school, I would oftentimes cut class before I fell too far behind because I could not keep up and I wanted to avoid being seen as "dumb." It all goes back to running away from that feeling of shame.

If I had suffered with ADHD as a child, it can be as debilitating to a child as molestation. In fact, both of these factors can leave a child on the outside looking in. Imagine having to deal with both simultaneously.

The time of year came when we had our class pictures taken. This would be my day to make a good impression on the kids in my class. It was my day to be on the inside! I dressed myself for school since my mom left early in the morning. I got dressed in my new outfit: a purple turtle-necked top with yellow flowers and purple pants. I cannot remember considering a mirror to check to see how I looked before I left for school, but if I did, I did not notice anything wrong. I happily walked to school among the other neighborhood kids—I couldn't wait to show off my new outfit! When I got to class, my teacher, Ms. Reynolds, said, "Your top is on backwards." I felt embarrassed; I just knew my outfit for the day measured up to what I felt everyone else had every day. All I could think of was how the other kids might have been laughing at me behind my back.

Anyway, we fixed the problem, and I went on to have my picture taken. I could not wait for the pictures to come back! When we finally got our class photos back, the first thing that I noticed was that my ponytail was not hanging like I thought it would be. As it turned out, my so-called ponytail was sticking straight up in the air! Just think—I was running around that day thinking I was "da shit." My turn to shine had turned into one of several shame-filled, humiliating, and embarrassing experiences that I would have as a young child. I am laughing my ass off right now! This story is kinda funny, but I definitely did not see any humor in this story back then.

For a long time, I felt that my parents did not love me enough, especially my mom. I did not feel special, I felt as if I were just "there." There is nothing like a mother's love. I do not remember ever being told "I love you" by my mom or dad until I was at least forty years old; it's all good, though, because today I know I was loved tremendously by my parents. My dad told me he loved me for the first time while he was battling cancer, and for the first time my mom said she loved me while she battled breast cancer. She and I had gotten really close at that time. Again, I understand today that my parents did not need to say one word to the effect of "I love you" because it showed through everything they did for my brother and sisters and me. However, as a child those things were not enough for me. I wanted hugs and kisses and to hear, "It's alright, baby."

GUILT, SHAME AND FEAR

A book of poems by Marian Foster Smith, *The Other Self,* is an amazing piece of work. I have found several poems throughout this book that put into words the feelings I know we all can identify with. This one directly unpacks the earlier paragraph:

The Mother Tree

"I am the Mother Tree, my dear, no other tree can give you as much as I. I give my bark, my timber and protection to all who come within my outspread arms. I give you my life-sap in the springtime, I give you leaves as covers for the fall, I grow in girth each year as does a Matron, I am the Mother tree, I give my All."

That is what I wanted. That is what my son would need years later.

By the time I got to junior high school (today it is called middle school), I had pretty much forgotten about my uncle. The feeling that I had done something wrong was gone. My hands did not smell nasty anymore. The little girl was gone. This was around 1975. However, the little girl with the smelly hands would arise again many years later. She would arise needing comfort and apologies. She would arise needing forgiveness. I would need closure.

Looking back on my childhood through junior high school, there were so many days when I wanted to be with the most popular crowd. I tried awfully hard to be a part of this "in-crowd." Perhaps I felt that being a part of this crowd was the only way to feel as if I mattered. I was always the third wheel, just tagging along behind them. I felt invisible most of the time, but I was okay with that because at least I was being seen by onlookers as a part of the "in-crowd."

I was not okay with being Pam Jones. Pam Jones was not smart. Pam Jones was not wearing designer jeans. She did not have money for school functions or spending money for class trips, she was dumb, and she was a virgin. The reason I mention that I was a virgin is because somehow, even being so young, I knew that all I had to offer was my body. She did not have a boyfriend like the other girls did. She was skinny with absolutely no curves. Pam Jones was still a five-year-old girl trying to be someone other than herself. This, on its face, may be quite trivial to most people, but I know there are more than enough people who know exactly what I am talking about. But why? Why didn't I want to be me? For me, it was because Pam Jones found out much earlier in life that she was not good enough, and she was not like everyone else. It was because Pam Jones had been emotionally wounded and unnurtured as a little girl.

Sometimes when I reminisce about some of the things that happened to me during junior high, I think about what others would say about what happened to me. I am almost certain some of y'all will say, "That kind of thing happens to everyone at some point during their adolescent years; it's no big deal." In a sense, they would be absolutely correct. However, the darkness underneath these adolescent woes for me was rejection and humiliation.

I took everything as rejection on some level. No matter how hard I tried, I would never be accepted by those I wanted acceptance from. I was accepted by what I used to call "dumb people." Yes, really. Keep in mind, I was twelve years old when I thought this.

This crowd consisted of people that were outcasts because they were not attractive or studious or they were shy or they too felt inferior, but unlike me, they did not appear to be one bit interested in the popular group of teenagers. The only reason I was able to blend into the popular crowd was because several kids in my neighborhood were a part of this crowd, so I got to tag along with them.

I believe that I tried so hard to be noticed by this crowd that I became an irritant to them, especially the boys. Have you ever met someone that you knew just wanted attention? Irritating, right? But even if my analogy was correct, I was too young to realize what I was doing, and I certainly did not know why. That is why being rejected hurt so much—because I did not know why I was being rejected; why couldn't they see that I was good enough?

GUILT, SHAME AND FEAR

The in-crowd consisted of the most popular students. There were the cheerleaders, cigarette and weed smokers, the sexually active, the drinkers, the partygoers and the well-dressed from the middle-class neighborhoods—the 90210's of the school if you will—and the kids from the projects who, in my opinion, were the leaders of this group. They seemed to be tougher than the kids that came from the middle-class neighborhoods. I am not sure why they seemed to be tougher than the rest of us. They were a closely knit community; I do not know about anyone else, but I always went out of my way to stay on their good side.

I tried bullying the classmates that I felt I could get away with bullying. I did not realize that I was bullying them. I did realize that this type of behavior gave me a sense of superiority. I would pick on kids that I knew would not fight back to create an image of toughness to the classmates I wanted approval, recognition, or acceptance from. Mind you, I was always one of the smallest kids in whatever classroom I happened to be in. That meant the kids I would try to bully were always bigger than me. What if the bullied kid had had the insight about bullies back then that the kids have today? "Punch a bully in the mouth as hard as you can, and you will never have to deal with him or her again." What would I have done? Because I was such a punk, I imagine I might have dropped out of school while I was in elementary school if I had gotten punched in the damn mouth!

Make no mistake about it: bullying is a cowardly act with potentially serious consequences for the victim. I hope that I did not have that serious of an impact on the kids I tried bullying. Hopefully, I was just an irritant they wanted to just avoid. The lack of nurturing, lack of confidence, and lack of worthiness at such a young age preceded my need for approval and acceptance; I used bullying to get all of these things.

I was twelve or so when I started to hide or shy away from crowds. I had become apprehensive about being around groups of people. My fear was that they would figure out that I was dumb or crazy or afraid.

I believed that people were capable of humiliating me, and the anxiety I would sometimes feel was at times debilitating.

Again, these stories may seem juvenile and "shit like this happened to all of us," but it was these kinds of things that affected this molested, focus-challenged, unnurtured kid very negatively.

I have a good friend that I met in junior high school, and we are still very close today; her name is Wanda McClary. Wanda and I have gone through a whole lot together since we graduated from high school. We spent a lot of time chasing rocks back in the day, which is all I will say about that. Anyway, I asked Wanda recently, "How would you describe me back in the day?" Here is what she wrote:

> Pam was quiet with a small circle of friends. Pam was cute and petite. Pam was a person, to me, who kept things to herself or let a lot of things go over her head. If she came to you with a problem, it was because she couldn't avoid it.

I will admit that I would "pretend" that I did not hear or understand something someone had said because I never wanted a confrontation that could lead to humiliation, and if I did respond there is a fairly good chance it would not have come out right because I would get nervous and start to stumble over my words sometimes. As far as being cute goes, as Wanda described, it never occurred to me that I was really cute. I have since realized that being cute or attractive is a double-edged sword. Being attractive sometimes gets the attention of those women who want nothing more than to fuck with you for being cute or attractive and the men who want nothing more than to fuck you because you are cute or attractive. Being cute got me a jealous boyfriend and a drug addiction.

Junior high school was a matter of me fitting in and being a "part of." At this stage of the game, a lot of kids began to go to parties and try out cigarettes, and Lord knows what else. I began cutting class and playing hooky from school. I began to feel as if I could make my own decisions on whether or not I needed to go to class or not; after all, my parents would never find out because after I got away with hooking class so much, I felt like all I needed to do was manage to pass most of my classes with at least a grade of C or D to be promoted to the next grade. I do not recall my parents even asking for a report card after elementary school. I believe my parents were only concerned that we finished school. That was fine by me, and I did manage to graduate.

Every girl who had a boyfriend was no longer a teenage kid, but "grown" in the mind of junior high school kids. You spent less time with the girls and more time with your boyfriend, the one who "loved you most." You were finally popular, you were a "part of" something— at least in my mind anyway.

I thought that if I took part in this type of behavior I would finally be validated. The cool kids would finally want to be friends with me. I would be accepted. I would matter. If I was popular, I did not need to be smart.

It was summer 1978. I was thirteen years old and about to enter the eighth grade. I was in love. My crush was the brother of a friend, of my best friend at the time, Wendy. Anyway, it was a summer romance, or so I thought. He was not the type to hang out; he stayed in the house for the most part. We kissed a couple of times. His mom worked, so their apartment was somewhat of a hangout for teenagers feeling their way through puberty. I made plenty of excuses for not wanting to have sex with him. My favorite was, "You can't handle this!" The real reason was that I was ashamed of my body: I had not filled out like the other girls who were definitely intimate with their summer flings. In the evening right before my fling's Mom came home, and everybody continued outside with their meaningless summer bullshit, I felt like a third wheel most times because my crush never came outside. I sat outside the apartment on the steps outside of his window hoping my "boyfriend" would come to the window to talk dirty to me.

Sometimes he did, but most times because Mom was home, he could not. When he could, after about fifteen minutes that would get old, he would leave the window, and I would just sit there until, eventually, the other two girls and their flings began to walk towards home. I lagged behind the couples who were walking slowly ahead of me; I was glad to be alone. The summer ended with my virginity still intact.

After the summer vacation, my crush started his first year of junior high school at the same school I attended. By the time late September came around, I felt grown enough that I was ready to have sex. My crush and I had not spoken much after the summer break, so when I saw him, I thought that he would be the one; after all, we did kiss. Of course, I could not tell him my plans face-to-face, so I decided to write him a letter and give it to someone else to give to him. Big mistake.

It was 3:00. School had just let out. Everyone was still hanging around the school talking, laughing, and waiting for a sister, brother, or friend to come out of the building so they could walk home together. All of a sudden, the boy I gave the letter to managed to get everybody's attention and read the love/lust letter I had given him out loud. I was humiliated. I never spoke to my crush again. I just knew that my class-mates continued to talk and laugh behind my back about the letter. The boy who read the letter continued to tease me constantly. There was nowhere to hide. I never cried, though—crying was a sign that I was hurting, and I would never ever let anyone see that what they did to me had an effect on me. To me that meant they had won, and their mission to humiliate me would be completed. I tucked the pain neatly inside of me until the day I could no longer take the pain anymore.

My third-period class in the eighth grade was science, if I remember correctly—another boring class that I probably fell behind in. I often hooked this class in the bathroom or just walked the halls unde-tected. At eleven fifty-five, I would make my way to the basement. The shop classes were down there, and so was my new love interest; the boy in the window talking dirty to me was ancient history. I had a huge crush on Renaldo, and he seemed to like me. He would often flirt with

GUILT, SHAME AND FEAR

me. He was so cute! And he had curly hair. Back in those days, curly hair was a definite plus! He was part of the "in-crowd." I would peer through the window of the classroom door just to get a glimpse of him. I would nervously and excitedly wait for the end-of-class bell to ring. When his class filed out for lunch, I would be waiting along the route I knew he would take just to say hi or possibly flirt with him. Most of the time he would give me a minute of his time. Some time was better than no time. I was so pressed. Anyway, I decided it was time for me to give in to what I knew he was into—sex. I said to him, "What is your address? I am going to come see you after school." He said, and I still remember this address to this day, "401 Q Street N.W." Yes! He gave me his address.

One of my friends from the neighborhood was Kim. She was a year behind me. I used to tell her that I was seeing this extremely popular boy. As a matter of fact, I used to make-believe we were girlfriend and boyfriend. All the girls knew him. I do not remember whether I told her that we were having sex, but knowing me, I probably alluded to the fact; basically, I lied. The day he gave me his address, I asked Kim if she wanted to go with me to see "my man." She said that she would go with me. We caught two buses. I was so excited. We got off the bus on Q Street and walked and walked. We asked and asked for directions to this address. There was no such address. He'd made a fool of me.

There was nothing I could do. I was rejected again. Kim never mentioned it again, at least not to me. Again, I never cried. How would you feel if you were in my shoes? Remember, I was a kid. I was internalizing all of this shit.

One of my best friends from the neighborhood was a cheerleader, so of course she was extremely popular. One day, I asked her to give my number to a boy I had a crush on (yeah, I had a lot of crushes). She said "sure." We were between classes; the hallway was packed with kids. I stood off in a corner somewhere to see his reaction when she handed him the piece of paper with my number on it. He was smiling at first—he thought it was the cheerleader's number. When he saw my name written on it, he threw the paper on the floor and walked away as if it were a joke. I was rejected yet again. I do not recall the cheerleader's reaction because I scurried away before the paper hit the floor, a sinking feeling in my stomach. Y'all, this is hilarious! I can assure you, I was not laughing then.

My mom began drinking a little heavier while I was in junior high school. The latest hairstyle was called a "snatchback"—the hair was cut shorter at the top of the head and got longer as you got closer to the back of the head, giving your hair a feathered look. My mom, with a glass of Brandy Alexander beside her, said that she could cut my hair into this new style. I wanted this style so bad I went against my better judgment and let her cut my hair. Before she was finished my dad said, "You done messed that girl's hair up!!" I slowly made my way to the mirror. I was horrified. *How am I supposed to go to school looking like this?* There was no way around it. I had to go to school.

I was teased so badly by one of the most popular girls in the school. She would laugh out loud at me, saying, "That looks more like a "snatchout" than a "snatchback!" As I mentioned previously, the incidents did not feel like just a part of growing up to me. It was not the fact that I had a bad haircut. It was the constant snickering as I walked by. It was the outbursts of laughter as I approached a group of students that hurt me so much.

The summer before my fifteenth birthday, Kim, the girl who caught the bus with me to see "my man," and I were on our way back to the neighborhood after coming from who knows where, when we ran into a girl from the projects. This girl apparently liked a boy from my neighborhood who was interested in me; I liked him too, but he was three years older and a lot more socially advanced, if you know what I mean. She joined us on our walk. The girl made a joke and I laughed. Not that it was funny—I did not want to not laugh at her joke because I was afraid of her. She stopped walking and said to me, "Don't laugh at my fucking jokes!" I mumbled something under my breath. Kim and the other friend of mine just looked at me. I felt like such a sucker, but

GUILT, SHAME AND FEAR

I dared not say anything. She'd humiliated me.

That would become one of many interactions I would have with girls from the projects, as well as girls from my neighborhood where I knew they did not like me, and most of them wanted to pick a fight with me. It was jealousy. I was cute. They all wanted that older boy who wanted me and who would eventually become my son's father, my first love, my introduction to drugs, and the first guy to physically abuse me. Those girls do not realize that they dodged a bullet.

I felt inferior. I was ashamed. I was angry. I knew my parents cared about me, but I did not feel loved by them. I felt I needed more of something I could not describe at that time. I wanted to be a good person. I wanted to feel loved by someone. I never fit in. I tried everything I knew to make people like me, but it seemed as though they never did. I never cried. This, my friends, is how my young life began. All I ever really wanted was to matter to someone.

THE GIFT OF REJECTION

WOULDN'T IT BE great if we'd had the wisdom we possess today when we were younger? If I had even remotely considered the sadness and pain of rejection as a gift, I would have been a bad sister! Unfortunately, the reality is that it does not work that way. Not only did I feel rejected when I was younger, but I also felt unloved or maybe even unlovable. Whatever the cause may have been, it did not make the feelings any easier to bear.

By the time the summer before high school rolled around, the molestations, the embarrassments, and the rejections of my adolescent years and my childhood had all been forgotten. My precious gifts were just beginning to bud. God had planned my life. He knew what was to come. He watched over me. He was intent on bringing these precious gifts to fruition.

For every person that suffers, you can bet your last dollar that Our Lord and Savior Jesus Christ is there. Every spiritually successful person would not have had this enormous form of success if not for suffering of some kind. Recall the suffering of Jesus Christ. He was crucified, but one of His many successes was that by suffering, He made it possible for all of us to have eternal life. For without Him, there is no peace.

Absolutely nothing brings us closer to God than suffering. If it were not, at least for me, for the gift of shame that I spoke about in this chapter, there is no telling where I would be today.

The painful gift of fear started to unwrap itself immediately after God eased the pain of the shame and humiliation that I had suffered throughout my childhood. It was not taken away, but it was eased just enough to get me through the fear of this next phase of the necessary spiritual bankruptcy that I would endure. Fear was sprinkled through-out my life, but the intensity was about to manifest itself, disguised as love.

Sometimes I look back on this chapter of my life and I can pin-point exactly where and when my life took such a drastic turn for what I believed to be undoubtedly the worst moments of my life.

I was still looking for acceptance, love, and admiration. Validation would become the most important aspect of becoming an adult for me. I still did not socialize well; I reverted to what I knew best—doing what my peers were doing. I was afraid that I would be exposed as being less than everyone else. I was afraid of being judged and teased by people. I had the tendency to say the wrong things or stutter over my words. Pam Jones was still controlled by the fear of what people could do to her verbally and physically. I had been groomed, by my own thoughts and the actions of others, to fear people up to this point, and years beyond.

It was the summer before I was to begin high school. I had fallen madly in love with "the boy next door." He was eighteen, I was fifteen. He had a job, a pool table, was popular in the neighborhood, plus he had a boombox. What more could a fifteen-year-old girl ask for? (LOL)

My first love was a lot more mature than I was. He was already drinking, smoking, and sexing. We spent a lot of time together. I would always peek out of our front door and windows to see him get off the bus or walking home from wherever he may have been. I stayed in the house most of the time listening to and singing love songs. There were other girls my age that wanted him, but he chose me. Finally, a man who loved me. I felt as if I was lovable and worthy to be noticed. I belonged to someone. But was it all too good to be true? Hell, yeah!

I lost my virginity to my first love on January 30, 1980. It was a Wednesday. I remember because I could sneak out of the house while my parents went bowling as they did on Wednesday nights. I was fifteen, and the result of losing my virginity was a terminated pregnancy. I had an abortion at the tender age of fifteen.

I remember afterwards feeling as though I was more like the girls I hung out with at school. I felt as if I belonged, I felt grown up, I felt normal. I had tried cigarettes in junior high school, but I never liked them enough to keep smoking. It wasn't until high school that I began to smoke regularly, just like the girls I hung out with. The first couple of years or so of our relationship were good. My parents still allowed me to see my first love even after I got pregnant. We were inseparable. But something happened. My boyfriend became very jealous, and he was totally against me smoking cigarettes. Looking back, I guess somehow when I began smoking cigarettes, some of my naivety or innocence was taken away, sort of making me just like my friends who had boyfriends and who smoked weed and cigarettes. One of my friends from the neighborhood had a two-year-old child already. Looking back, again, he probably saw that I could be influenced by someone other than him.

Less than six months earlier, prior to my "coming out," I did not have a boyfriend; I did not smoke or drink, and the thought of ending a pregnancy was unimaginable. If my boyfriend did believe I had lost my innocence, I guess he was right. Before I graduated from high school there were several incidents surrounding my boyfriend that should have opened my eyes, but I was blinded by the fact that "he loved me."

My first love and I attended the same high school; I was in the tenth grade and Andrew was in the eleventh or twelfth grade with a half-day schedule—life was perfect. We held hands as we walked together in the halls or outside of the building; we always had lunch

GUILT, SHAME AND FEAR

together too. Like I said, nice.

In high school, it was an all-day occurrence for quite a few girls to meet in the girls' bathroom for one of several reasons. One, to smoke. Two, to fix your hair or put on makeup or lipstick. Three, to cut class. I had begun to pick up where I left off in junior high school; I was not a studious person, and I couldn't keep up with my studies. I would always start off every year with the intention of doing well in my classes, but I just could not keep up. The one exception was my sewing class. I loved sewing because I could make cute outfits. I loved fashion then and still do. I had always been better with my hands—in part, because it meant that I could work independently without the fear of judgment. As I mentioned earlier, it was quite possible that I suffered from ADHD, and my other classes didn't grab my attention quite like making my own clothes. Essentially, I would just stop going to classes and find myself in the restroom or outside the building somewhere with others like me.

One day, while I was in the restroom doing Lord knows what, guess who came through the door? Yes, my boyfriend. He pulled me out of the bathroom by my hair and forced me into a corner out of sight of everyone, and he choked me. I had scratches on my throat where his hands had been. I honestly believed that he did it because he cared about me so much that he had gotten violent. I was sixteen years old.

By my junior year in high school, my boyfriend had dropped out and decided to go to night school. Now I could smoke as much as I wanted to without the fear that he would find out. But just in case he showed up, as he did from time to time, I always kept double-mint gum in my bag to freshen my breath.

Remember my friend from junior high who was a cheerleader, the one who gave my crush my phone number? Yeah, her. She was a cheerleader in high school as well. She lived on the next street from where I lived. One afternoon at 3:00, when class let out, she and I were offered a ride by one of her fellow cheerleaders and her boyfriend. Coincidentally, the other cheerleader wore glasses and wore her hair in a mushroom just as I did (I wore that mushroom for damn near ten years or more!). Anyway, when we got to my friend's house, I got out of the car with her instead of having them drop me off on my street; my first love and I lived on the same street. When they pulled off, they drove toward my street, and I began my walk to the next block to my boyfriend's house.

As I approached my boyfriend's house, I saw that he was standing on the front porch. As I got closer, I could see the look on his face—a look that I saw many, many times. A look I would never forget.

He said to me, "I saw you in the car with that nigga."

"What are you talking about?" I asked. "I just got out of the car around by Lisa's house." He did not believe me.

I went inside his house as I always did after school, and he followed me inside. I sat at the dining-room table. I remember him standing behind me on my left side. I heard a click and then the smell of something burning—I realized that he had set my hair on fire. I frantically patted my hair because I thought my whole head of hair would catch fire; thankfully it didn't. Later, he said, "I didn't mean to."

Again, I was convinced that the reason he was so jealous of me was because he loved me so much. I did not realize at the time that these acts were a form of control.

The summer after I graduated from Anacostia High School was the best summer ever. I did not go out and there was no school. My boyfriend didn't have anything or anyone to be jealous about. I was all his. That is, until cocaine arrived in our community in 1984 to join our relationship.

GUILT, SHAME AND FEAR

THE JOURNEY TOWARD
SPIRITUAL BANKRUPTCY

I GRADUATED FROM high school by the skin of my teeth. To this day, I do not know how. Years later, when I decided to go to college, I had to get a copy of my transcripts only to find my grades were devastating. I was reminded of how much I'd missed in terms of my education. All Ds, and maybe one C.

About two months after graduation, I got a job. My mom had given me her old car, a bright orange Chevy Chevette—you couldn't tell me shit! My first love and I were more in love than ever. My mom and dad were proud of me. I was going in the right direction; this was 1983. In March of 1984, I got pregnant. By November 1984 my first love had made himself scarce, and by December 1984 my son was born. By the summer of 1985, I was a full-blown addict and alcoholic.

We were inseparable for the first year or two. We went everywhere together on the bus, and sometimes Andrew had borrowed his sister's car. We went bowling and to the movies. We visited his brother who lived in Mayfair a lot. I loved going there to play Pac-Man; I was fifteen and this was around 1980. We were the epitome of teenagers in love, which is a sickening kind of love.

When I started my first job in June of 1983, I was introduced to the "fling"-at-work routine. The majority of my coworkers and I were all right out of high school. The relationship I started at the time was new and exciting and seemingly better than the relationship I had at home. Nelson had become my new first love. I was so in love with this guy. He was the cutest guy on the job in my opinion, and obviously this opinion was shared by several other women at work too. I'm sure most of you can relate to this statement: when you start a new job, you become "fresh meat" to the guys working there. Y'all know I'm right!

I was Nelson's latest conquest. The fact that I worked the night shift was a plus because he would come to the job damn near every night during my lunch break. He was nice to me. The first and only Christmas we would share, he bought me a gold necklace and bracelet, which was all the proof I needed to realize that Nelson cared about me. I would not go so far as to say he loved me, though. I found out after about a month or so that he had a girlfriend at home. I could not be mad because I had someone at home too. I was good with it. After a while Nelson began to lose interest in me.

I moved on to someone I had met through a friend at work almost immediately. After about a month or two I realized I was pregnant with DJ. I was not sure who the father was, but common sense told me that one of my first loves or the third guy I met at my friend's house in 1984 was possibly my son's father. The third guy was convinced that the baby was his, and to be honest, I was not completely sure. Back then not many guys asked for a DNA test. It was accepted that if you were a couple the baby was "obviously" his; luckily for me, as the years went by my son began to look just like his father.

I stopped seeing the third guy while I was pregnant, but as soon as I had the baby and went back to work, the relationship between the third guy and I resumed because my son's father apparently did not want to be in a relationship anymore and I didn't know why.

I believe I kept seeing the third guy because I just wanted to be wanted, but something was up with him—he kept disappearing and leaving me in the house with his family. He never got to see my son, by the way; my baby wasn't his and I was sticking to that. I found out the reason why he kept disappearing: he was on crack. That relationship ended, and a relationship with my own crack addiction would begin soon enough.

On December 27, 1984, I was at home. Andrew was at his house with a friend. I assumed that they were getting high on something. At around 4 o'clock that evening, I started having pains. I called him to take me to the hospital, but he never came even though he was only four houses down from me. My dad and mom took me to the hospital only to be told that I was not ready yet—my water had not broken. I went home, my water broke the next day, and my parents took me back to the hospital around 5 o'clock. This time it was time.

I did not see my first love the whole time I was in labor. I lay on the bed watching the intensity of the labor pains on a monitor until the time finally came to push. I remember being hot as hell! Where was he? About five minutes before my son was born, I saw him standing about ten feet away ready to pass the fuck out. Our son was born at 9:54 pm on December 28, 1984.

I was taken to my room at Washington Hospital for Women and anxiously waited to see my son. When the nurse finally brought him in, I was in disbelief. *Wow, I am a mother; this is my son.* It was surreal. We were discharged two days later. My son's daddy picked us up.

Before I got comfortable with the idea of being a mom and bonding with my son, postpartum depression kicked in. My boyfriend was very inconsistent in visiting us even though we were, again, just four doors away. My desire to spend time with my baby's father increased. I loved my child, but I often felt that I was not doing a good job taking care of him because he was always crying. I wanted my relationship with my boyfriend to go back to the way it was before I got pregnant.

Unfortunately, it did not work that way. My hope while I was pregnant was that as soon as I had the baby, we would get close again. It appears he did not feel the same way. It was around this point when I resented being a mother. It had become an obligation. As I write this sentence, my heart sinks, and my eyes begin to water. *Oh my God, how could I feel this way about my precious son?*

I am getting off track here for a moment, y'all; we will pick up Andrew in a sec, but I need to say this right now. There is a memory that rips at my heart: My son had gotten into my sister's seizure medication. Somehow, he had gotten the top off of the bottle; the pills were spread out on the carpeted floor surrounding my baby. I put my finger in his little mouth: there was a single pill, so I took the pill out of his mouth. I could not be certain if he had swallowed any of it; he was acting normally to me. I was on crack at the time; however, I had not smoked any this day and I decided to be "Mommy" for a change and take my son to the playground. However, I did take a couple of Schlitz Blue Bulls with me for the outing. My son was fine the whole time we were there, but when we got home, I noticed that he could not hold himself upright. I knew this was more than him being sleepy or tired from going to the playground. I suddenly realized this was a reaction to the medication. I took him to D.C. General Hospital. They kept him for a little over a week. I would visit, but certainly not like a mother should have. My son's hospital admission gave me time to be the crackhead that I had become. My son's hospitalization provided me with an all-day-and-night babysitter. I didn't have to lie to anyone or pick him up from anyone or explain where I had been to anyone.

I had my most recent sugar daddy take me to visit my child again for a couple of minutes; I don't know what the hell was going on with me and Andrew at this time. As I left the infirmary that housed these beautiful babies, all in cribs, I turned one last time. My son, standing up with his tiny hands holding the crib's wooden bars, looked at me as if to say, "Mommy, where are you going?" or "Please don't leave me here alone again." I ignored his silent plea and continued to leave my

GUILT, SHAME AND FEAR

son. My son was no more than three. To be completely honest, I tear every single time I play this story in my head. My God, please forgive me.

Going back to my first love, I felt betrayed and disregarded by my boyfriend. We had a child together. We were supposed to be a family, but my son and I seemed to be merely afterthoughts to him. I was disregarded because I did not fit in with his new friends and his new pastime. I decided that I would go to him. My son and I began to spend more time at my boyfriend's house. I met some new faces and connected with some neighborhood folks that I previously had not had conversations with—just "hi" and "bye"—mostly because they were all older than I was.

I do not recall the exact day I found out why he had these new relationships, but I remember clearly what happened the night I met the first of many people who were cocaine users, including longtime neighborhood friends; I had no idea that they were indulging in the use of this hard drug. I knew that damn near the whole neighborhood either smoked weed or drank alcohol around this time, but I was somewhat shocked by the cocaine usage. Not that I judged them. It was just that cocaine, to me, was something white folks used. Ultimately, cocaine would be the demise of all of us.

One night, there were three of us in the basement of my boyfriend's house—me, him, and a visitor from Florida who was related to the next-door neighbors. I had seen him a couple of times over the years but had never actually met him until that night.

Long story short, they were snorting cocaine. I was invited to take a snort and I loved it. In a matter of months, I was hooked on powdered cocaine. We spent every dime we had on cocaine and Reunite wine. We must have gotten an income-tax check or something because during our new pastime we moved into our first apartment, but two months later we had to move out for not paying rent; we moved back into his mom's house. My son was nine months old. We both had gone from snorting cocaine, to cooking cocaine, to smoking crack. Essentially, I had gone from wine and powdered cocaine to crack and cheap beer. I had also begun to steal from my family. By June or July of 1985, I was a full-blown addict and alcoholic. I was admitted to my first rehab that same year. Whatever innocence I thought I had was gone.

The journey toward a new and better me would be a long one. So much had to happen for me to get to where He needed me to be. I would not change one thing—no, not one. I blamed my first love for a while, but it did not take me long to realize that this was my problem to solve. I understood that we were both incredibly young and were ill-equipped to handle the grown-up emotions that go along with being in any relationship, especially when drugs were involved. He never knew about my childhood; he never knew how emotionally damaged I was. I had no idea why he was the way he was. Maybe it was because he did not have his father in his life, or maybe he felt that I belonged to him and was only able to display control disguised as love. Our relationship never had a chance to develop because drugs had taken over us while we were way too young. Drugs and alcohol turned us both into something we were not.

This book is in no way meant to embarrass or make my first love feel guilty about anything. Today, we are good friends. We genuinely care about each other. He has a new family and is a great dad. He has apologized to me for everything he put me through, and I sincerely accepted. However, this is my story, and he is a part of that story.

If it never rains, then how will we learn to appreciate the sun? We may feel defeated and weak sometimes, but those things that make us feel defeated and weak help us to grow spiritually. Never be afraid to say, "This is what they did to me," because when we talk about how situations and circumstances made us feel, we release the pain we have been carrying all by ourselves for so long. Damn right—let it all go! It's okay, baby. But remember, not everyone is going to like it or agree with it; choose who you release your pain to carefully.

GUILT, SHAME AND FEAR

WILL THE PAIN EVER END?

I HAD COME to realize that alcohol not only helped neutralize the effects of crack cocaine, but it made it a lot easier for me to socialize. Increasingly it became a need more than anything else. Every relationship I had for over twenty years, minus the thirty-day stints in rehab, included both drugs and alcohol.

Relationships served several purposes for me: to solicit drugs, alcohol, attention, and validity. Damn near every dime I made from work was used to support a substance abuse habit. If the "relationships" couldn't get it done, then certainly "tricking" would. I would never admit to myself that I was prostituting; it hurt too much. I would meet these men and sleep with them for about a day or two. I had convinced myself that I wasn't tricking; I mean I knew them, they weren't strangers, per se. *I aint no prostitute*, I thought.

I drank to the point of blacking out, vaguely remembering how I got where I was.

Even if I had remembered, I needed to remove the scene from my mind so badly that I talked myself into believing that "it's no big deal" or "I am the only one who knows." Let me tell you something family, being the only one who knew, was not a luxury; it became a shameful act I carried around my neck for a day or two and then buried along with all the other shit. Shame.

My appearance started to decline. I was already petite, but when crack took hold of me, I became downright bony; my cheeks were sunken. The infamous crackhead—dirty scarf on my head and all. Look what I had become.

I worked at a mailing service that was in Lanham, Maryland—the place where I met Nelson. This was also the place where I had to endure humiliation and judgment on a higher level than my adolescent years due to my first black eye. My first love assumed that I was cheating, and he beat me.

This time I was cheating with this guy at the mailing service. Even though my first love didn't know for sure, I knew I had cheated, so I guess I believed I deserved what he had done to me. After that first black eye I became angry, but also afraid, if that makes sense. I would never allow any man to control me or shut me up. Rebelling against him made the beatings more severe, but I learned that fighting back was my best choice—sometimes I got him off me. Often when we had an argument, it turned physical. I refused to let him win. I refused to allow him to think that beating me would ever shut me up. All that said, the emotional and mental toll was severe.

I sported two black eyes at once on one occasion. I was choked to the point of passing out. I was choked and had to fake like I was passed out to get him off me. Once, I had to get stitches in the temple of my head because he had pushed my head into the corner of the iron railing while I was sitting on the porch. The doctor explained how lucky I was, telling me that one half inch to the right and I would have been dead. This man beat me or we fought on a regular basis. I had somehow become used to having black eyes. I acted like the black eyes were not visible through my eyeglasses. But you know what hurt me the most. It was the verbal abuse, not the physical abuse. He would regularly refer to me as a bitch and I hated it, but oddly enough I just got used to that too.

I did not love him, but my self-esteem was so low that I felt that I could not do any better. After all, who wanted a crackhead?

My dad was disappointed in me, and I assumed that my siblings were ashamed of me. I was ashamed of myself. In a little over a year, I had experienced what it was really like to be in despair. I had become so anxious, worried, and unable to get a grip on my clear emotional demise. Crack cocaine and alcohol regulated every aspect of my life in some way, shape, or form. The worst part of it all was that I had become hopeless.

Thank God for my family. My family looked out for my son. My family loved him when I could not. If it were not for my family and his dad's family, the odds of CPS taking my child would have been imminent.

I checked into Mountain Manor Treatment Center in 1985 with the help of my wonderful mother, and thirty days later, I was refreshed. I had gained weight and was extremely attractive (in my eyes anyway). My plan was to continue drinking but leave the crack alone—for good. The real reason I went to rehab was not to stop drinking and drugging, but to get away from the fighting and all the negative outcomes created by my drug use—the arguments and fights, the lying and stealing, the tricking, the judgment and the humiliation. I needed peace. I was becoming emotionally unstable. I wanted to be able to use drugs safely because I had no idea how I would get through one day without a crutch. Think about that statement for a minute. Thirty days later, on the way home in the van provided by the treatment center, I said, "Driver, would you be able to stop at the liquor store?" I picked up where I had left off almost at once.

I struggled to be a decent mother. I was only employable for months at a time and I awakened with the shakes every morning, anxiously waiting for the corner store to open to get a beer and a shorty.

I covered up my relapse for a while. I kept my job, managed to sublet an apartment from another crackhead, and still managed to hold on to my looks. When you feel as if you have nothing else to offer internally or otherwise, the external part is all that is left for you to give. But that, my friends, will cease to exist sooner rather than later. My friends in Alcoholics Anonymous call this person a "dressed-up garbage can." I dressed up the outside of myself. I was still looking for love in all the wrong places. I was still looking for someone to love me or validate me. I didn't even love myself.

I cannot begin to count the number of men I slept with, the number of men I might have introduced to my son. They were all older men I could count on for either drugs or money. These men were at my beck and call. All I wanted was a relationship that would validate me because I did not know what real love was, and I certainly knew that I was never going to love any of these men. They genuinely professed to love me; I used them and left them without a second thought.

Some of us will settle for the first thing smokin' just to be able to say that we have someone who "loves" us. A relationship for me was just another form of masking my low self-esteem and low self-worth.

My first love and I grew completely apart by 1990, but we had remained get-high partners. We both knew that we were seeing other people; he knew about most of the relationships I had had, even the white guy I was seeing—that's a story for another day. As a matter of fact, my first love was seeing numerous women who lived in the same community as I did, Benning Heights. That hurt a li'l bit, but I would not give him the satisfaction of knowing that he was hurting me.

Even after we were no longer a couple, he still felt the need to come to my apartment and put a gun to my head. "I am just playing. It's not loaded," he said. I knew this was yet another scare tactic. I was not fazed at the time, but looking back at the incident, it could have ended my life. It's all God—it had to be.

I decided to go to rehab again in 1995 because I was tired of the way I was living. I was tired of looking ugly, tired of the real or imagined judgment of family and friends, neighbors, and coworkers, tired of barely surviving. I knew I was better than the crackhead and alcoholic that I had become. My sisters and brother moved out of the house and were living their lives. I was envious of the normal lives they were living.

When I got clean in 1995, I decided I wanted to have a normal life like the other folks I knew. They were getting married, buying homes and cars, but most of all, I wanted their drug-free lives. I was thirty years old by this time, and I was craving peace, love, and success of some kind. My first love came to visit me once while I was in rehab this particular year, only to have sex with me. He had started ignoring the many phone calls I would make to him while in rehab. I remember telling him how much I loved and missed him; he was telling me that it was pretty much over. I was hurt. Here I am trying to get clean to become someone that he could love again. It was obvious to me that he was seeing someone even before I went to Mountain Manor for the second time, but I figured when I came home it would be different.

When I came home, I was still living in Benning Heights. I ended up having to leave the apartment that I'd subleased from my crackhead associate and got an apartment in my name. Andrew did not want to commit to living with me and my son because he did not want to be obligated in any way with paying his own way, and he could see whomever he chose. Andrew chose to live with his mother.

Once again, I came home from rehabbing looking good. I guess he noticed too. He moved in and by September 1995, we got married.

I needed someone to do my hair for the ceremony because I did not have a lot of money; Andrew recommended some girl he knew that did hair. I had seen this girl before, but I only knew her as a friend of one of his friend's girlfriends. The day before the wedding, I went to get my hair done by this girl; after I had my hair done, his friend's girlfriend admitted to me that my fiancé was seeing the girl who had done my hair! I was angry and hurt that he would do such a thing to me. I let it go; after all, I was the one he was marrying. I asked him about it when he picked me up, but he denied it.

Andrew did not come home that night. I waited nervously for him to come in the morning because we had an appointment to get married. He finally showed up smelling of alcohol in a gray suit with a black shirt, no tie, and several buttons unfastened at the top, looking like someone straight out of a *Scarface* movie. The day just went downhill from there. We argued, the car broke down, and I spilled spaghetti on the off-white dress I borrowed from my friend Wanda. My son was with us. That was the day I relapsed again.

My drinking got out of control again, and once again, crack became the companion of my drinking. Physical along with emotional abuse made life for me, sometimes, very dark.

Of the seven days of the week, it was often the case that I would have at least one day of peace; not peace of mind because it was always in the back of my mind the fact that my life was in shambles and that I was on the lowest part of the scale that is society, but on Sundays it was a little different in that I did not wake up in the morning wondering how I was getting to work or how I was going to get high when I got off work or what the fuck we were gonna argue about tonight, if I saw Andrew at all. I guess what I'm trying to say is that there was a period of normalcy on Sundays. I would drink on Sundays, but the strong urge to get high when my beer kicked in was dull. Sundays always started out as family day—at least for most of the day. I would get up, clean the apartment, go to the store and laundromat and prepare a Sunday meal with whatever money Andrew and I had left over from Friday— normal stuff. On Sunday I felt like myself, I was Mom. It seemed like things were good, but then the evening came and reality set in again: I only had enough money to get to work for one day and that was Monday; I would figure out how to get home later. Week after week, year after year, there was always a storm brewing.

GUILT, SHAME AND FEAR

THIS KIND OF LOVE IS ......

THE FEELING YOU get when you find yourself walking slowly along the almost empty street in your neighborhood on a fall morning—the sun shines brightly, the leaves are so beautifully colored, the air slightly cool on your skin, but storms are in the forecast.

The feeling you get when you squeeze your child so tightly, with the warmness of love only a mother can give, and your child says, "Mom, I can't breathe!" through unmistakable laughter, but unexpectedly they are hospitalized, and you cannot touch them.

The feeling you get when you fall in love in the springtime, but months later you are left alone, in the freezing cold of winter, by this kind of love.

This kind of love leaves us wondering, why?

This kind of love leaves us wanting more of something that cannot be controlled by the forces of nature.

This kind of love makes the goodness of love vanish.

This kind of love, for some, is the first love.

I wrote this piece of literary work in 2017; it was copyrighted in 2021 to encapsulate a moment in time. A fleeting moment of light amid so much mental darkness. My first loves—Andrew, crack, and alcohol—consumed my soul and spirit, leaving behind the true love of God, my child, and myself.

I didn't know this then, but I know it now: God had not let me down before this and He darn sure wasn't gonna start now. My God has always protected me, despite the harm I and others did to me.

AND THEN, GOD SENT HIM

BEFORE WE GO into this chapter, I need to tell you that this part of my addiction involves a lot of my boyfriend/soon-to-be second husband's life too. That said I will not get into the weeds of my addiction over those years, to protect the privacy of this innocent bystander.

From 1996 through 2003, my addiction had taken another route this time, but I was headed for the same turbulent destination.

I relapsed less than six weeks after leaving another rehabilitation center. My addiction summoned me to continue the journey toward spiritual, emotional, and physical suffering.

I met the man who would become my second husband, Ronney, in May of 1996 while I was still married to my son's father.

I had gotten another job at another mailing service. This type of job was somewhat physical, and you are required to stand for eight hours, minus the half-hour lunch, sorting and bagging or boxing mail while operating the machinery that produced the mail I sorted. The setting was that of a warehouse. This was the kind of employment I had through my entire addiction. I was good at it, though, and it kept me employed. The mailing service was in Rockville, Maryland. Typically,

I would catch the subway to work, but this day I had no money to get there; I had not gotten a paycheck yet. My brother Jun worked in Rockville and offered to give me a ride to work. I had relapsed again by this time but my brother didn't know that I had. I was early into my relapse and was looking pretty good. Of all days, my second or third day at my new job, the car breaks on the Baltimore-Washington Parkway. My brother's good friend, my knight in shining armor, showed up. My knight in shining armor would have to come to my rescue many, many more times. He was in for seven years of pure hell.

I hid my crack addiction from him for as long as I could—or at least I thought I was hiding it. Years later, he informed me that he knew all along, but he did not want to believe it. He did not want to believe that the woman he fell madly in love with was a crackhead. He knew I was a "heavy drinker," but stopped short of facing the fact that I was an alcoholic.

He tried taking me out of the 'hood. He tried spoiling me. He tried introducing me to "normal" living. I wrecked his cars. I stayed out all weekend without so much as a phone call. This man would have to pick me up from the police station after I was pulled over for drunk driving. Eventually, he had to drop me off at the jail so I could serve my ten-weekend sentence.

I showed no regard for his feelings. I disrespected our home. I lied to him so many times it was pathetic. I will not get into the particulars of the occurrences over the seven years of hell I put this man through, but this man stayed with me because, he said, "I see things in you that you don't even see in yourself." But that didn't stop him from getting so emotionally sick that he was prepared to leave me. I tear up every time I think about what I did to my husband. I loved him, but because of my addictions, he and everyone else would always take a backseat.

Ronney saved me from a lot of the consequences of addiction for a while. I often wondered how I was able to snag this loveable, kind, and considerate man. He showed me that I was worth loving.

I did not believe that he saw good in me. I did not love myself. I was still a little girl living in a grown woman's body with no idea how to achieve security, love of self, or true love of others. I was an addict faced with pretending to be all these things. My soul and spirit had been broken, my mind was filled with self-doubt and fear. The little girl in me still yearned to be nurtured, but she just watched from inside of me as the spiritual turmoil raged on. She was alone. I felt alone. Have you ever felt alone in a room full of people? That was the story of my life. In March of 2003 I got clean again; this time there was no rehab, this time I broke down. I was tired of "hiding" my addiction, I got tired of lying to my significant other, I got tired of hurting him, I got tired of all of it.

It started out like all my Friday paydays. I would get picked up from work by a crackhead male friend of mine—yes, just friends. I had my own money and he was more of a damn crackhead than me! Plus he was always somewhat drunk or high when he picked me up; the majority of these times he would even try me. He was irritating as I don't know what, but he had a vehicle.

We went to a crack house that we had visited before. Same ole routine. Get high, get drunk, run out of money, buy stuff on credit from the so-called dealers in the house, and when that ran out we sat and looked crazy, wondering who would come through the door with more drugs.

My friend often rented out his car and the dealers always came back—except for when they didn't. This night/morning they didn't come back. My friend decides to go looking for his car. I don't know if he found it but he never came back. Friday turned into Saturday, Saturday turned into Sunday, and Sunday turned into the wee hours of Monday morning.

I kept peeking out of the window shades: no sign of him or anyone else, but the snow had started to come down hard.

I sat down in one of the filthy old stuffed chairs again; the house was quiet with the exception of for the other crackhead, she lived in the house—she was still geekin'.

I knew there was no way to get home, and once I got home what lie was I going to tell? I had no money—again.

I began to cry without making a sound. I prayed, "Lord, please get me out of this chair and out of this house." I tried to get up, but I couldn't. I prayed the same prayer again. I got up and looked out of the window and went back to the chair. I begged, "Lord, please." I got up and walked out of the house, into the cold, snowy, and early morning, with nothing.

I had stopped crying, but I was anxious. I remembered seeing a fire station a bit down the street. My plan was to ask for a ride home from someone there—yes, that was really my plan.

I knocked on the door; when the fireman answered the door, I burst into tears. I was sobbing. "I am an addict, I need help." They didn't take me home to sober up—they took me straight to the emergency room!

As I lay on the stretcher in a quiet hospital room, my anxiety passed. I was going to be okay, just needed to think of a lie. I didn't even get the thought out of my mouth before the hospital staff came in and wheeled me out into the hallway. Now, everybody and their momma was walking by me. I was afraid someone would recognize me, I looked like I spent the last couple of nights in a crack house.

I forgot how I got home, maybe the bus. When I got home Monday morning around 9:30, I knew my significant other would have left for work already. To my surprise his car was still parked outside.

I walked in the house and saw what appeared to be his bags packed, by the front door, but I didn't see him anywhere. I hurried back to the bedroom to prepare to take a shower before he got back from wherever he may have gone. Suddenly, I hear a muffled sobbing coming from the walk-in closet. My 6-foot 4 man was sitting on the floor of the closet crying. He said" I don't want to look at you looking like "that" anymore and why didn't you call. I would never call. He was constantly worried sick about me. But he never cried, or I had never seen him cry. He was leaving this time. There was no time to plan to go to another rehab. From that moment I knew God was working on my behalf. I quit that day, never to take another drink or drug. Alcoholics anonymous was the solution for eight years.

No matter the cause of our emotional pain or mental anguish, real or imagined, it only takes one person to make a difference in the life of those who suffer from pain in any form. All of us want to feel as if we matter even in our darkest hours. However, I still felt empty. Something was amiss. A connection to spirituality, a connection to a higher power, I would find years later, was the key.

THE LITTLE GIRL IN ME

I am another you.

I am flawed.

I went from being a molested child to enduring the shame associated with the challenges I had staying focused, to rejection and insecurities, to physical, emotional, drug and alcohol abuse.

The little girl never stood a chance. She never got a chance to grow beyond being a little girl.

Being clean at this point in my life was good, but the real truth is that I was still the same little girl living in a grown woman's body. I had become arrogant and self-aggrandizing, I felt like it was my fucking time to shine. I had learned long ago how to dress up the outside to hide what was going on inside of me.

I would dress in the sexiest clothes I could find, six-inch heels, a nice car and stride in my step that just wouldn't quit, at least in my eyes anyway. I would draw all kinds of attention from men. It was my appearance that gave me the courage to fake like I was so confident. I didn't have to speak one word, I let my looks speak for me and it was this persona that several women I associated with could not stand but I didn't care, "they just jealous" I would say to anyone who would listen.

Today, in the year 2022, I still love sexy clothes and nice cars but this time I am confident in my ability to accomplish whatever God has planned for me even without dressing up the outside.

Have you ever had a family member or someone you knew dress or act in a way that was contrary to their age? For instance, there was a guy I knew from the neighborhood that always dressed nicely. He was about twenty-years old at the time. He wore cornrows in his hair, and he talked using the slang of the time. He used to be a small-time hustler with a blinged-out car. On all accounts, at least as far as he was concerned, he was living his best life. The year was 1990. Do you know this guy is now sixty years old, has the same mentality, and acts the same way even now? It appears to me, and I have heard, that we stop growing when we come to the point in our lives that is most comfortable for us, mentally. It is a serious struggle to move beyond that part of our lives because we are uncomfortable with what lies ahead.

Around 2008, my husband and I lived in an apartment in New Carrollton, Maryland. It was a two-bedroom unit. I got clean in 2003, so this was several years later. I decorated our second bedroom. The furniture was white, the bedding was of lilac and yellow flowers, with stuffed animals resting on the fluffy pillows and the carpet was light blue. I thought my bedroom was the most beautiful room I had ever seen. The little girl in me always imagined having the life of the three girls on the TV show, *The Brady Bunch,* the room was decorated very similar to Marsha, Jan and Cindy's room.

I recognized that the little girl in me still existed the moment I completed decorating the bedroom. I thought she had grown up and was okay...we were okay. She still needed to have her comfort zone, her hide away, a place she could thrive at her own pace and not the pace society would have it. I was comfortable in the bedroom.

My husband saw the room and said to me, "This looks like a little girl's room." I did not realize throughout the few months I spent decorating the room that the designer of that room was the little girl in me. I was forty-two years old.

I worked at an area hospital in 2008 on the night shift. My coworker, Bobby, and I used to have deep conversations. I am not sure what the topic of our conversation was on this particular night, but Bobby said to me, "Pam, you are like a child." He was not being insulting. I believe it was just an observation that could not be ignored. I sat at the nurse's station wondering what I had said to prompt this response. We talked a lot about my past. It is likely that the little girl was doing all the talking.

My life was going as good as I had expected it to go, and the little girl kept her place within me I was okay with it.

THE BEGINNING OF THE END

BETWEEN 2008 AND 2010, there were many of life's most painful yet invaluable lessons that would let the air out of my bubble of sobriety without inner change.

My mother-in-law moved in with us. My husband lost his job of twenty-five years due to the financial crisis throughout the nation in 2008. I had to get rid of the dog that I had for five years, my baby, Laramie. Finally, we had to move out of our apartment because we just could not afford it anymore, we could not make ends meet. We moved into an apartment that a family member could no longer afford. We took over the lease.

I was angry and bitter but dare not give up on my newly found success of being drug and alcohol free, working full time and going to school. I even started hanging out with my family every weekend, something I had never done during my battle with addiction. Another blessing for me was the fact that I had gotten sober before my first granddaughter Ke'shannah was born in 2009, she never saw grandma drunk or high and I was proud of that.

In January 2010, we were finally able to get a place in my name in the same complex as the apartment we sublet from my niece. Life was better because of it but I was still angry, and I felt overwhelmed, but I can't pinpoint the reason I was overwhelmed. As the months had gone by the urge to drink had gotten stronger and stronger. Someone had given us a gift basket for Christmas that year, the gift basket had a seven-ounce bottle of wine, it sat in the back of the refrigerator for weeks. I relied on self-will to keep my head above water, and to maintain my sobriety, because at this point spirituality was not a priority in my life, I didn't need it. After all, I was handling all this shit just fine.

As it turned out I wasn't handling shit just fine, I relapsed in January 2011 two weeks into the new year. "The wine bottle was frosted as it sat on the desk within arm's reach as I sat at the computer. My husband asked from behind "Do you think what you are about to do is alright?" I answered "yes". At that time, I was more concerned about my eight-year streak of being sober would be ending than the danger of a trip back down crack lane. Me, smoke crack, never again.

In the back of my mind, I had a bad feeling about what I was about to do but maybe, this time, I would be able to drink like a lady.

I popped the top and Satan walked through the door he had been trying to open since 2003. I had blocked out what I knew about the disease of alcoholism; it is cunning, baffling, and powerful.

All I knew was that it was the best tasting drink I had ever had! The very next morning the spiral began to take shape faster than the eye of a hurricane. I found myself at the liquor store for "something small," like a four pack of the same bottle of wine I had taken out of the fridge the day before. This was the beginning of the end of my career as an addict.

Some days, I would rationalize to myself that if I did not do any crack, I could consider myself a social drinker because it never failed, drinking alcohol of any kind led me to the crack pipe or crack stem. Maybe this time I will be able to "drink like a lady" I mean after all, I still had a job, a husband, a new car since I had wrecked the car I had just made my last payment on because I blacked out behind the wheel of my car and as far as I knew no one else knew I had relapsed, again.

I felt that if I could pull off being a social drinking my life would be so much better. I never did get to drink like a lady and being a drinker of any kind was out of the question. This time around I added a few things to my resume of destruction: a DUI, weekends in jail, the privilege of having to take a urinalysis every week, a totaled vehicle, a probation officer and more self-degradation.

This cycle of insanity lasted almost a year to the day that I picked up the seven-ounce bottle of wine. I had hit a wall again. My job was in jeopardy, my marriage was not in jeopardy, but it was not good. I began staying out well into the wee hours of the morning again. I worked the night shift at the time and on an occasion or two I went and got drunk and high instead of going to work. I would hang out with women and men the entire night, go broke, feel depressed and guilty and then go home after the hour my husband went to work. My husband didn't know I was not going to work but he did know that I was spiraling out of control. The time had come when I could no longer run away from whatever kept me drunk. I needed help.

I decided to take a leave of absence from work, which meant I had to admit to my boss that I was drinking again after I had bragged to a degree that I was a recovering addict and that I had been clean for eight years. At the time, my sobriety was the icing on the cake I cherished just to be able to say I am a survivor of the streets, somehow, I thought my co-workers would look at me as a strong woman. I was still looking for validation.

My husband watched me self-destruct. He began to avoid me most times, but he still took care of me, he buried his resentments. He was in pain. He had to watch his wife, who had been clean eight years self-destruct again.

The rehabilitation center I went to this time was out in the damn boonies somewhere. My husband drove me to my new home, for thirty days, while I tried to sleep off the previous night's high. I was in bad shape y'all. My hands were shaking so badly I could not hold the utensils to eat my food, I couldn't even sign my name on the admission papers. I was tired mentally and physically. My husband could breathe a small sigh of relief knowing I would get the help he had been encouraging me to get for months. He was as mentally tired as I was. After detoxing for seven days, I was able to start my recovery again. This time around I knew with every fiber of my being that I would never drink or use crack again. My husband needed his wife back and I needed my life back.

I joined AA in 2012 after a year of pure hell, and I have not looked back, thank you Lord.

The constant need to function as an adult while the inner soul of the little girl was active was difficult to pull off a few years ago but not today. I realize that most who know me or knew me would agree that the little girl in me is alive and well. I am not sure whether folks feel sorry for me or not, but at this point in my life, I am confident, kind, and unselfish and I can honestly say "I don't give a damn". I embrace the fact that I am a woman and that a little girl lives in me. A little girl lives in every woman to a degree, and it is not a terrible thing. I tend to embrace her a lot more now that I have come to recognize she exists. I am not afraid anymore, so I do not care too much anymore about what folks think of me, but I do care about how I make others feel. Sometimes I feel as if I live my life nurturing the little girl that felt she was unlovable. I am giving her a voice. I am giving her all the love she did not get so long ago. Period.

"Women and girls can be vicious," my husband quoted his Aunt Rita. It appears there is always a competition of some sort between women, me included. There was a time in my life when I was envious of other women. I would have a tough time being happy about another woman's success. I would never acknowledge their accomplishments; at times I would chalk it up to "luck" and not arduous work. The fact of the matter is that when we judge other women on their accomplish-ments, looks, personality or anything else, there is something in this other woman that we lack in ourselves. We tend to secretly wish for one another's failure. It does not matter whether she is family, friend, or foe. All that matters to any woman with insecurities and low-self-esteem, such as me, is the failure of other women, with the primary goal of self-elevation.

My life was not all bad. There were times in my young life when I was okay with being Pam Jones. My family life was better than most in that I had both parents in my life. Both of my parents worked hard to make our home a home. We had nice Christmas holidays. We had meals every day of the week. Sunday dinners were always great. We had structure, we had rules and consequences if the rules were broken. I believe that it is these things that we take for granted when we are young that make going through a difficult time doable. I guess what I and my siblings had was a solid foundation.

Now that you have read parts of my story, you heard straight from the horse's mouth how personal challenges and the actions of those we meet, has the absolute ability to affect us mentally and emotionally for years. Let's talk about the key to overcoming all those negative aspects. Let us talk about God and spirituality. Let us talk about inspiration, endurance and overcoming.

THE SPIRITUAL JOURNEY

GOD IS PERFECT in all He does.

We ask ourselves, if this statement is true, why do such horrible things happen to us? Why is there no justice for our offenders? Why did I have to go through so much emotional pain and anguish?

I am not a religious or spiritual scholar by any stretch of the imagination. It is because I survived all these things that has made me a believer in a power greater than myself and that Power is perfect. Every day we awaken is another day we have survived the night. Every day we awaken is another day for us to do things differently.

When we are enduring so much pain, it is extremely difficult to see how God is at work on our behalf, but He is. Vengeance is His. Not only that, but the injustices that befall us only serve to bring us closer to Him and to totally depend on Him to guide us through all phases of life.

Suffering is one of the greatest teachers there is as it relates to our relationship with a Higher Power. Just look back over your life for a moment. Remember everything that He has brought you through. Here is another thought—what about the things we cannot see that we may have been saved from. There is a reason we get delayed sometimes in our daily quest. It is my belief that our lives may have been spared from whatever evil or unintended consequence that may have come for us on that day, at a particular time. There is a reason we did not get the job or promotion we knew for sure was ours for the taking. It is my belief this position/promotion would sidetrack His purpose for us. There is a reason it all fell apart. It is because he, she or it was not good enough for us. We go through a lot of emotional suffering to keep a personal relationship with others from ending but it is destined to fall apart if God knows it's not in line with His purpose for us. God gives us free will to do whatever we want but if it is not in His plan for us, no matter the extreme measures we use to manipulate the outcome, it's not going to happen. Period.

Along with suffering through toxic relationships, which in turn, leads us to seek a Higher Power, another aspect of healing through suffering is through seeking perfection. There is no such thing as perfection among the humankind.

I used to feel I needed to be perfect in everything I did during and after my addiction. The reason I used to feel this way was because I convinced myself that because I was an addict, I had to do everything perfectly to avoid further condemnation. The reason I believed I needed to be perfect after my addiction is because I was still insecure about my place in society, I felt like I was behind my peers as it pertained to financial and educational security. I had to work harder, speak better and dress better than those I worked with. This is called keeping up appearances.

I used to want to change who I was because I believed being like others would be more acceptable, but to heck with that, if I am being someone else, who the heck is going to be me? There is only one me, and the best person for the job is guess who—me. That said, there are things about me that needed to be addressed like egoism and arrogance. That is where spirituality comes in.

The maintenance of spirituality is an ongoing endeavor, but well worth the price of admission. With spirituality comes peace, hope, and a better understanding of how God works on our behalf. Remember the battle is His, not ours. That is a comforting thought for me. When our souls become permeated with so much negativity, our spirits suffer. We become distant from our natural, loving selves. We distance ourselves from the Lord and Savior without a second thought.

Growing up, my parents made us go to Sunday school and church every Sunday even though they did not go themselves. The older I got, the more I hated going. I remember thinking that when I got old enough to make my own decisions, I would never go to church again. I would go on special occasions like Christmas and Easter, but that was it. By the time I was twenty years old, I had completely blocked out the notion of a Higher Power and church on any level.

I believed that God would only help those who praised Him, those who went to church every Sunday, and those who sinned less than me. I used to believe that I had to stop using drugs and alcohol for God to listen to my cries for help. I had sold my body and my dignity to the Devil. I was not worthy of His love or protection. I believed that I deserved all of the pain associated with emotional and mental abuse brought on in part by my addiction. I constantly condemned myself. There are a countless number of us who can relate to this level of condemnation and thereby making spirituality seem unattainable.

Condemnation is the work of Satan. Condemnation causes us to despair. Satan does not want us connecting to our spiritual selves because that means his hold on us loosens. Another fact is that Satan is a liar. God will accept us no matter what we are going through. God is constantly holding out His powerful hands for us to grab on to. God has never, or will ever, leave us. Keep striving to be the best you that you can be and leave the rest of the battle to Him.

No matter how far down the scale you think you have gone, God wants you to come back to Him. His whole plan for you is to make you in the image of Himself. He is fighting for you even when you cannot feel Him near you. Remember, just look back to the tough times, when you knew that you were not going to make it through, you will be so amazed at what He has already done.

NO MORE SHAME

IF LEFT UNTREATED the remnants of being ashamed are bound to show itself in our DNA, somehow. Fear of being shamed or being ashamed of ourselves can lead to other types of fears. Shame keeps us from living a good life to some degree. We become afraid of failure and success because "when" we lose it, the shame we will endure leads to the fear of being exposed as a failure in the eyes of society, which includes family and friends. Also, with shame comes condemnation, and that my friend is a tool of Satan.

Shame has a way of causing us to hide from life. When we are ashamed, we open the doors to feelings of being unworthy of love, success, and any meaningful relationship.

When I began authoring this book, I would ask some family members about shame. Ninety percent of the time, most would not speak on it, or they just deny ever feeling ashamed about anything. However, one person, my battle proven, Aunt Carol spoke about it.

May 5, 2018, the day of my cousin's wedding. There were four women having their make-up done. I thought it was the perfect opportunity to ask them what their feelings were about shame. I read to them the first paragraph I had written about shame. They all agreed that the paragraph was spot on, but the room fell silent when I asked them to talk about any relationship they had with shame. It was not the perfect opportunity that I had thought. Someone in this group may have been still ashamed of themselves about something and as a result, they hid from the opportunity that may have opened the door to the healing process.

My Aunt Carol responded, "Ain't no shame in my game." How many times have I heard and said those exact same words? Those words say that I have been ashamed for so long, that I have gotten used to the feeling. I got used to feeling inadequate. I hid behind the persona of being unabashed. However, in Aunt Carol's case, she meant exactly what she said because my aunt had overcome so much of life's many obstacles that there was no place for shame to live anymore.

A March 16, 2017, article in *Psychology Today*, by Neel Burton explains that shame is a response to something that is morally wrong or reprehensible, and that it is worse if it is exposed, but unlike embarrassment, shame also attaches to a thought or action that remains hidden from others.

The article goes on to say that people with low self-esteem are far more prone to shame. Also, in the same article it says, "shame derives from, to cover," and is most often expressed by a covering gesture over the brow and eyes, a downward gaze and slack posture". Also, shame and guilt go hand in hand. Guilt is, "I did something bad," and shame is, "I am bad." Shame is about who we are. Guilt is about our behaviors, explains Burton.

I was between writings and decided that I really needed to be more informed educationally and not just emotionally informed about shame. The more I delved into educating myself on this emotion, I realized that there was more to overcoming shame than I had initially thought. Don't get me wrong, I still believe to a degree that experience is one of the greatest teachers, but the question of how to overcome shame still lingered in my mind. "What is the cure?" So, to speak.

I want to share with you, my discovery. I hope you will find this information as helpful as I have.

I wanted to come to you with "experication" (life experience), but I also know that there are others who have studied the topic of shame and have also studied all that ails our spirit, a major step in the right direction.

Brene Brown, Ph.D., L.M.S.W is the author of a book I read called *The Gifts of Imperfection*, Hazelden Publishing, copyright and published 2010. This book helped me with being okay with being an imperfect me, not that I could ever be perfect, but I could embrace the imperfections I believed I had. Brené writes that courage is the most important quality that wholehearted people have in common. The definition of courage that she talks about is ordinary courage and not the old definition that has us to "speak one's mind by telling one's whole heart." The meaning of courage has changed. Today's definition is that courage is more like being heroic. She says, "heroics means putting our life on the line. Ordinary courage is about putting vulnerability on the line.

Pages 38-47 of *The Gifts of Imperfection* are about shame resilience. The text on page 38 supplies an insight on three things that you need to consider about shame.

First, we all have shame. The author explains that shame is universal and a primitive human emotion, the oldest emotion that there is. People who lack empathy and a connection to humans do not feel shame. That sounds like a narcissist to me. I am very blessed to say that I do not know of anyone personally who fits this description. I believe that narcissism accounts for a small population of our society.

Secondly, we are all afraid to talk about shame. I had that sense when I asked the question about shame when I visited my cousin who was getting married.

Finally, Brené says, "The less we talk about shame, the more control it has over our lives".

On the other side of the spectrum, after a decade of research, she

GUILT, SHAME AND FEAR

talks about the elements that people with shame resilience have. They understand shame and recognize what messages and expectations induce shame for them, they practice critical awareness by reality-checking the messages that tell us that being *imperfect* is being inadequate, they reach out and share their stories with people they trust, they speak shame—they use the word, they talk about how they are feeling, and they ask for what they need.

No matter what stage of the shame game you find yourself in, you can overcome it. Understand that you are imperfect in a perfect way and embrace your imperfections; it's okay. Shame is just another way for the Devil to keep control over us because if we are ashamed of ourselves, then it is almost impossible for us to seek a Higher Power, and that is playing right into Satan's hands. You are special, you are smart, you are worthy and most of all, you matter. Don't you forget it!

I pray, "Lord thank you for holding my hand the whole way through, even when I did not deserve your Grace and Mercy. Thank you, Lord, for turning my shame into a magnificent vessel that has found its way toward You."

LIVING WITH GUILT

WHAT IS GUILT? Why is it so difficult for us to admit that we feel guilty about something? According to *Psychology Today*, guilt, like shame, embarrassment, or pride has been described as a self-conscious emotion, involving reflection of oneself. Meaning, that this feeling is brought on by us, internalized by us, and kept by us.

Guilt is an offspring of condemnation. When we admit that we feel guilty about our actions or how our actions have affected someone else that means we are taking responsibility for the outcome of a particular situation, or at least our part in a situation. That was a hard pill for me to swallow because I did not want to believe that I was the cause of my son's pain.

Perhaps we did not help someone, and that person ended up in a dire situation. Perhaps we did not answer our phone when we saw that it was "him or her again," and that person ended up hurt, or even worse, dying. Maybe we did not keep a promise, and because of our broken promise, someone was left heartbroken.

Throughout my life, I have often considered myself to be one of those women who were not nurturers. I could not recall a time

I really felt like I was a mommy. It hurt me when, in my mind, I was incapable of loving my son the way he should have been loved. I carried that in the back of my mind for years. However, while I had to recollect this time in my life for this book, I had the most cherished memory I could have ever had.

I used to work the nightshift at my first job. In the morning, I would hurry home to see my son, this happened pre-addiction. I ran up the stairs to my mom's room to find him lying on the bed, looking up at me with the most amazing smile. He was so happy to see his mommy! I remember feeling like this is the one person in the world that loved me more than anyone else on the planet. I tear up just thinking about it. I could love my son and not just taking care of him. I was his mommy. I really loved my little boy. Unfortunately, that would probably be the last time I had that feeling for close to twenty-five years. My addiction began in 1985. My son was born in 1984.

During my addiction I somehow managed to cloth and feed my son with the help of my family. His dad and I made sure he had all of the newest kid favorites but nurturing my son was elusive, disciplining my son was inconsistent. One occasion of discipline comes to mind. I even went to his elementary school to check up on him a couple of times like a concerned mommy would do, I was slightly buzzed. The teacher noticed that I was peering through the classroom window of classroom door, I motioned to her "shh". DJ was acting a fool! I entered the classroom in my semi drunkiness and embarrassed my child by beating his butt in front of his classmates.

I did find out years later that someone other than myself or his father was interested in educating my son, the drug dealer. Sadly, outside of that I do not recall anything I had done to ensure my child was being educated to help ensure he had a shot at a fruitful life.

There is so much of my son's life that I do not recall. I found out years later that my son was on the basketball team in elementary school. I didn't have a clue. This was abandonment and neglect.

When I met my new boyfriend. I moved out of the apartment I shared with my first "husband" and my new boyfriend, and I moved in with my aunt in 1997. . . without my twelve-year-old son.

I left my son in the hands of his addicted father. When that did not work out, my son lived with my mother until me and my new first love moved into our own place in 1998. By this time, my son was thirteen or fourteen. I enrolled him in school in New Carrollton where we lived. He did not do well. He kept getting into trouble and hooking school. I had relapsed in 1997 and was still actively in my addiction, so I threw up my hands and sent him back to his father. I used to pick him up on the weekends, but the older he got, the more he would rather stay in the neighborhood where his friends were and there were few rules. I stopped coming around, for the most part, which is why I had no idea that my son had dropped out of school after junior high school. I was free to do whatever I wanted to do. My son and his father clashed. My son told me after many years that his dad physically abused him. My son even went as far as to threaten his dad with a gun.

My son was sixteen or seventeen in 2003 when I got clean, again. I remember going to my ex-husband's house where my son stayed until he moved in with my mom again. With tears in my eyes, I begged my son to forgive me. He said he did, but I do not think he could forgive me at that time. After leaving my son at the most critical ages of his life to fend for himself, there was no way this kid had anything but resentments toward me. I cannot say that I blame him.

It was not until well after I sobered up that I would finally admit I felt guilty about my son's life taking many of the same turns as mine. My son would lash out at me saying, "It's your fault that I am this way!" Not only that, but he also told everyone who would listen to him that because of his mom and dad, his life was messed up. I tried to make amends, as I was recommended to do in Alcoholics

GUILT, SHAME AND FEAR

Anonymous, but I would never admit that I was part of the reason my son's life was full of chaos and self-destruction. Making amends for me meant saying, "I am sorry for how your life turned out," but I never took responsibility for it; I would never admit my guilt. I would never admit that I felt guilty about anything because I knew if I admitted that I felt guilty, I would have to take responsibility for the outcome. I had enough problems of my own, and to think that I would take responsibility for "his" problem was not in the cards. That is how it was for me as it related to my son. I was busy with my own life—my own existence is probably more on point. I had gained some things during my eight-year sobriety run, so feeling guilty about what I had done to my son would negate the "success" I thought I had. My friend, Lisa, said to me once, "You are an arrogant ass." I did not think I was at the time, but there may have been some truth to that statement.

My addiction began when my son was no more than a year old, however, during his childhood I did not realize that I was neglecting my son because my son never wanted for anything. His dad and I bought him stuff that few kids in our neighborhood had. Those other kids, as it turned out, had something my son did not have—an ever-present mom.

I tried to "make up for lost time" between 2003 and 2012, as it relates to my son, but it was not until 2015 when I began to feel guilty about how my son's life was changed by the decisions I had made. Did anyone notice how little I mentioned my son in the first part of this book? The only time I mentioned my son in length was the time when, "I looked back at my baby, and my baby looked at me. I was leaving him behind, in a crib, while he was in the hospital. I left that poor baby alone to wonder where I was going".

By the time my son was around four or five, I made the decision to leave him motherless on countless days and nights. I made the decision to flaunt strange men in my child's life. I made the decision to drink and do drugs in our home. I made the decision to expose him to a life that was filled with negativity. However, the most damaging aspect of my guilt was that I did not show my son the love and affection that only a mom can give. The love of a grandma, auntie or uncle is imperative, but nothing compares to the love between a mother and her child. My child did not get the nurturing he probably craved. When I realized this fact, my heart broke into so many pieces. I did everything in my power to get rid of my guilty conscience. My thought was, if he succeeded in life, the condemnation I carried around because of guilt would disappear and we both would live happily ever after. The road of condemnation I was on would last for years. Eventually, guilt and fear would team up against me.

Conviction is an offspring of repentance. I was in so much emotional turmoil. Pain was the motivator that turned condemnation to conviction and repentance. When we are convicted, we have taken responsibility for whatever we have done and only then are we open to the idea of repentance. After years of failed attempts at "saving my son," I had no choice but to hand my son over to the care of God. It was then that I realized that I had transitioned from condemnation to conviction.

I am going to share with you portions from my very first journal. I began the journal on February 3, 2015, the year I began to deal with all the damage my addiction had caused. I hope it will convey in real time, the painful revelation that I was, in fact, responsible for the way my son's life had turned out, even though I never openly admitted it. I was under constant condemnation by none other than myself.

The entry, May 8, 2015, is the beginning of the guilt and fear journey I had found myself on, but this is also where the idea of God began to materialize. The idea of this Higher Power became tangible.

I thought that because I had gotten sober, my life would

automatically shift from being tumultuous to being calm and full of successes. The successes came, but calm and peace were elusive for several reasons. First, removing drugs and alcohol from my diet was only a drop in the bucket as it pertained to being mentally sober. Secondly, my mind still had not transitioned from the noise of my past to the great future I had imagined. In other words, I still had the same mindset I had about life as I did while I was in my addiction. Finally, spirituality seemed to be hard to obtain. I knew I wanted to be closer to God, but at the time, my need to change the belief of those who knew me, the addict, was more important to me. I still chased validation. I opposed anything that would hamper my progress, such as admitting I was responsible for the way my son's life had turned out. I buried the way I felt so deeply, I convinced myself that the feeling of guilt was not real.

After a year or two, I was finally able to come to grips with the fact that I felt I was guilty of creating the storm that had become my son's life, even though I know today that God saw things differently. I had to go through this life-changing process. The good news is through this process, my belief and faith in God started to manifest itself. The other aspect of this process—fear.

Fear became a significant factor after I assumed that I was guilty. At times, fear would become literally debilitating. I feared for my son's life and that if, God forbid, my son lost his life, it would be my fault. I turned to weed until weed turned against me.

Prior to starting my journal there were many incidents that happened between 2009 and 2015. Prior to 2009, the year my granddaughter K'eshannah was born, I thought that all was well with my son. He had a job, a car, and the love of my mom and dad. Not that I did not love my son, but at this point he seemed to be doing ok, and he was twenty-five years old. The year my granddaughter was born, my son began his journey of many encounters with law enforcement. Strangely enough, my storms began after my first child was born too. It was after the birth of my second granddaughter, Tondelia, when I started to see the constant disruption of their happiness and the detriment to the safety of my grandchildren.

The court appearances, writing letters to judges, jail, probation, domestic violence, property destruction, fights, public intoxication and coincidentally—K-2, the newest drug to destroy the Black community, had arrived and destroyed as many families as crack did to our communities in the eighties.

My son's life had become my life. I spent a lot of money trying to keep my son from despair. I spent a lot of money trying to fix what I had broken. I believed my son over his children's mother. Big mistake. I wanted him to keep his kids in his life. His children loved their father a great deal, so the thought of separating them from him was hard for me to grapple with. I remember how happy they were to see him when we picked them up from the court building for visitations. I wanted my family to survive this difficult time, I needed for him to succeed as a father. I did not consider the damage my son was causing my grandchildren and their mother. I did not believe my son was all the things my daughter-in-law accused him of being because I had yet to see for myself the behavior that my son displayed, I did not want to believe it. Sadly, she was one hundred percent correct, and I was one hundred percent wrong. She said he was violent when he was on drugs, and she did not trust him with the children. My grandkids' mom put up with my son's addiction and abuse. She had become me; we were both victims of the father and son duo. How could I not see this when it was happening?

She fought hard to protect her children from their father. Not that he was physically abusive toward them, but because he was emotionally abusive to them and often left them vulnerable to outside danger when he was either high or drunk. My grandkids loved their father, but they were afraid to be alone with him, and they were justified in their fear.

It was a holiday. I am not sure what holiday it was, but the girls were with me. I allowed my son to take the girls with him to the old neighborhood to celebrate. When he left my house, he was sober. I

GUILT, SHAME AND FEAR

had learned the lesson months before that I would not hand them over to him unless he was sober. In fact, it had been a good week or so that he had been sober. Hours later, a friend of my son brought the girls to my doorstep. My son had passed out drunk, leaving these two little girls unattended—again. That is when I knew I would never hand them over to my son, whether he was sober or not, without my supervision.

My son lived with my mom for years. Every month or so, the police came to her house. He would be drunk. He would argue or tear up the house. The police in Charles County knew my mother's address by heart. He went to jail several times, thirty to ninety stents vowing that, "This is the last time." The last time never came. I would send money for jail stuff, toiletries, and telephone and video calls for the girls. Every time my son found himself in trouble, I would be the one to suffer with the financial burden of "saving him" from the dire consequences of being institutionalized. I was afraid for my son. I was afraid that if I did not minimize the consequences, my son would not survive.

One day, I received a phone call from my son's best friend, the same one who brought the girls to my doorstep during the holiday. My son's best friend had moved on with his life, leaving my son behind. It had been years since they had seen each other, so it was pure coincidence that my son's friend had come across my son, literally. He told me he found my son laying on the sidewalk, people were just stepping over top of him. My son was on K-2, a synthetic form of weed used by a lot of Black men and women at the time because it could not be detected in the urine, making it ideal for those on probation as my son was. This drug was killing him. I left my house crying. I was on my way to yet another scene, and I was sure I would see a sheet covering my son. I was driving along Southern Avenue in Washington, D.C., trying to get to my son. Suddenly, something said, "Go back home." I never made it to the scene. I found out hours later that he got paranoid and jumped out of the ambulance half naked. He did not even know who his best friend was. His friend called me and told me he was finally taken to the hospital. I went to the hospital only to find out he had left the hospital. I panicked. Fear gripped me so fiercely that I curled up in my recliner and begged God to save him again.

The incidents I have just laid out were the norm. I was fearful damn near every day, from 2010 to 2015. I had to let go of guilt and fear and let God. Fear was seeping into my veins.

FROM THE PAGES
OF THOUGHT

I AM GOING to pick up the story in 2015. Keep in mind the following pages are quoted directly from of my journal, there are some grammatical and punctual mishaps I decided not to change. I wanted it to sound as real as it was, if that makes sense. All right y'all, let us get started.

May 8, 2015, 7:11pm
What a day! DJ started using that crazy stuff again. He was seen in two different hospitals on the same day. He didn't remember most of it. Anyway he "promised" me that he would never do that crazy stuff anymore. Yeah, ok we'll see. Didn't take him long maybe two hours. I feel so bad for him. I don't understand why he is afraid to face life's ups and downs. He just wants to look stupid and not know what is going on around him. It's soooo sad. I hope he makes it to GW with me, sober. I am gonna pray and try to let it go. It's hard, I love my son. DJ needs help. DJ needs to change everything about himself. Fear. 721pm. (notice the last word in this entry).

JUNE 8, 2015, 4:00pm

A lot has happened since last time. DJ damn near killed himself using that "Scooby "stuff. Prior to that he manages to be considered for a job at GW! I don't know if he's learned a lesson this time or gotten scared enough by this bout of insanity. He says he has. I'm scared. I don't like to answer calls because I'm scared somebody gonna say your son did this or that or your son is dead. I found myself trying to get closer to my higher Power. I want peace. It's not DJ's fault its mine. I have been trying to practice "acceptance". Sometimes I do well other times I can't say I really even consider it. I do know that those times I get it right are the best! 4:16pm

August 31, 2015, 4:14pm

Wow. Sometimes I can't believe how my Higher Power knows what I need at all times. It's been a pain filled and challenging past couple of months. A lot of growth too. I don't think I've ever sought my Higher Power like I have recently. Through family arguments and the fact that DJ is still holding on but barley. I'm afraid to even answer the phone most times for fear of another argument. Hate filled and angry. Or just plain fear. I prayed and prayed, and cried and cried, seeing only brief seconds of peace. My attitude has been very angry. It seems like life is so unfair. Which I now realize is not so. Life is just the way it's supposed to be at all times. Easier said than done. Today I got what I perceived to be just what God says it's time for me to have. DJ found someone that he really loves. After months of being turned down by bad news from GW DJ may start on September 14. (Notice here that I have claimed my son's happiness as my own)

My husband used to tell me that DJ is a grown man and to stop getting so involved in his life because when I get upset, he gets upset. Essentially, while I was busy trying to "make up for lost time" my husband was forced to watch me suffer with what he knew I was going through, a guilty conscience.

December 31, 2015, 1:25pm
It has indeed been a long while since my last entry. Quick update.
I have been on an absolutely tremendous journey. Spirituality! Still
smoking weed every now and then. I no longer beat myself up
about it either. I am not dependent on it. If, or when it becomes a
habit. I'll talk about it at that time.

Through His word I have been able to live fear-free for the most
part. DJ doesn't have a stronghold on me anymore. I'm not afraid
for him like I was. Don't get me wrong, I still have days of fear but
nothing like it used to be. I'm so happy and thankful to have found
what I call "peace and serenity". God has been so good to me. I
had been reading a lot about spirituality, fear, anxiety, worry and
anger. I even went to see a shrink!! I still have a ways to go but I'm
so glad that at least I've started on a new approach to life. I don't
do as many AA meetings as I used to, probably because I'm smoking
weed, but AA has been my salvation and path to God. Guess what
I bought my first Bible today! I'm so excited! No plans to bring in
the New Year yet." 1:42 pm Thursday.

Trying to manage guilt and fear, as it pertained to my son, was
like a roller-coaster ride—the cars make their way towards the sky by
way of very steep tracks, and then suddenly the cars plummet to the
bottom. Then the cars easily and calmly glide along leveled tracks and
come to a complete stop. The complete stop is when God takes over. I
stepped aside and stepped into spirituality.

I have learned that even though I may not live the "perfect" sinless
life, I am worthy of God's love, God's blessings and a peace that only a
connection to God can give. The maintenance of spirituality is a lifetime
commitment of progress. It is okay to have tiny increments of success on
our journey towards peace of mind and spirit. Remember it is a process.

By 2016, my life was going in a direction that I could not have
imagined. I was still entrenched in the notion I could save my son from

his, in my opinion, deadly path. I was caught between spirituality and my earthly self. I wanted to save my son more than I wanted to trust God to save my son. It took a lot for me to move forward with bettering my life, in that, I struggled to enjoy the successes that only God had given me. There were times when I had to force myself to rejoice about what God was doing in my life because I felt I was not deserving of all God was giving me. I needed for my son's life to get much better before I could settle into God's plans for my life and until that happened, I could not be truly thankful to God for my new life. Sounds like I was still dealing with a guilty conscience.

All right yall, lets continue with the journal.

Wednesday Jan 20, 2016
Going to my first Toastmasters meeting!
Friday Feb 4, 2016, 317pm
Life is good. I formally joined Toastmasters International Wednesday. One of the projects is to give ten speeches to other members, one of which is to be videotaped! OMG. My faith in God is growing. Faith will have to keep me going in this endeavor. DJ is doing ok. Still working. I have to believe that he's doing the best he can at any point in his life. God's got him. I bought a notebook so that I can start putting my speeches on paper. Haven't thought of a name yet but I definitely know it's going to be about fear. My life had been based on fear so long before I recognized it. I have to stand in front of one of the things I fear most "people" and give a speech ten times for starters. I'm excited and overwhelmed at the same time. I'm changing yall. Read all types of books mostly spiritual but I am also reading "How successful people think" Hubby just came in. Till next time. 3:34pm

Friday 21 342pm
Today was a good day!
I had been fretting over the pursuit of my God given purpose. I asked God to please, yet again, show me I'm moving in the way

that pleases Him. Went to an AA meeting today I raised my hand to share. I shared some of what is going to be part of a series of speeches. People responded overwhelmingly! I read my Bible this morning. I love it. My mentor expressed that I have a natural voice to become a very good motivator! More confirmation from Him! I listened to my playlist and my Manhattan's Cd. Have not done that in a while. Feels so good. Took my baby his lunch. A great day. Thank you Father 350pm

Wednesday Feb24 2016 3p
Gave my first toastmaster assignment! It's a speech. Those people were speechless! A couple of them said my speech was powerful. Can you believe DJ wanted me to cancel my speech just to take him to the DMV! He said" Ma leave them people alone" I told him how selfish he is. It kinda hurt my feelings that he doesn't feel that something I had been talking about for months meant nothing to him. He failed the test and for whatever reason he was unable to get money out of the bank. I called him the other day just to see if he was ok. He pretty much told me everything was ok and that he could run his own life now. Cool. He went on to say "I'll call you if I need you. I don't think he meant it in a nasty way. His new girlfriend Tinna was there, we were on speaker. Maybe they had discussed how "your mother trying to control your life". Which is probably true. So I'm fine with stepping back.

I called him later that day to see if he got the money and if he passed his driving test. No answer. Donna told me afterward that he failed, and he was angry. So I'm assuming that's why he didn't answer. I will be so glad when he stop smoking that shit. His outlook on life is very negative. Still blaming others. I'm worried about what he'll do today. So, I'll pray to God for him to be ok. DJ has been a major player in my relationship with God. Is that strange? When I worry about DJ I get closer to God. I love my son soooo much and God knows this so whatever happens in DJ life

is good for both of us! We both learn a lesson. I know I do. DJ a
little slow but he'll be fine. We are getting a new bed today $1800!
Ronneys idea. Let me get back to making spaghetti 326pm.

March 16, 2016
After a couple weeks of confusion, pain and anger DJ then gets his
"valid" driver's license. The next day Tinna bought a truck. The
next day he crashes the truck at 6:30am with the girls in the truck
with him. The police called me. The officer said he did not call it
in but suggested that someone needs to talk to Mr. Jones. He was
drunk or high or both. I laid him out! He hadn't called me for a
week prior to this. I was hurt. I kept texting him a bunch of times.
A week later, another incident. He missed Keshannah's competi-
tion. Fast forward, today he called, he was sober, expressing how
messed up his thinking is, he now realizes he needs to change. By
the way, he called while on his break from community service.
After all that mess, he had put us through this past week, I have
been praying and hoping that something big would come out of
this storm. It has!! It just seems different this time. I think he is just
about ready for the pain and anguish to stop. I love God! He's so
good to me. Plus…HE is using my son to get through to me. I know
HE wants me and DJ to be happy at last. We are His children. I'm
so proud of DJ right now. No, not proud of him but happy for him.
I still pray for him I've been in the place that he's in. Its really dark.
I am thankful that my son has, if only for a short time, found a
moment of peace and clarity. 719pm

There were regular seasons of low-lows and high-highs. I was getting tired of my peace and happiness being dependent upon my son's
life. At this point, I didn't know whether God was directing me or
if guilt was directing me to suffer when my son suffered. I will say
that whatever the driving force behind this roller-coaster ride may have
been, I felt I needed to go through this with my son. I often thought

if I had put the time and money in when he was younger, I would not have to do it later. In essence, blaming myself again.

The purpose of exposing parts of my son's life is not to make him look bad. As I have explained to my son, the purpose of the journal entries is to let others know they are not alone in dealing with issues of guilt about our children. The mental anguish and fear we suffer during this phase of our lives can be overwhelming, but necessary. The other reason is that even if we do feel guilty about any of our actions or inactions, we can learn to be okay with those actions. If we view our guilt as a road map to spirituality, then guilt has served its godly purpose. I hope you will see as you continue to read parts of my journal that the journey to spirituality is ongoing, but when you get there, it is well worth any guilt, shame or fear that I could have ever endured. Let's move on.

MARCH 24, 2016, 3:10p
Gave another speech at Toastmasters yesterday. Paul and Aref came to me after what they called an amazing, powerful, dramatic speech. Aref said "Today you are in the right place at the right time!" OMG!! After the speech "all" the members were blown away. They said I need to start making money. I still can't get over this shit. God's hands are all over this! Imagine, me, an inspirational speaker on somebody's stage!! I'm so grateful. I'm gonna follow every bread crumb my Father lays! I believe, I believe, I believe! 318p Oh I forgot, Aref gonna set up some meetings with some influential people for me. OMG! OMG! OMG! 319p

This was one of the most exciting moments of my life. I was overwhelmed with joy. I never followed through with Aref about the meeting with the Pastor of a historical church in DC. Fear kicked in again. Even though I knew the possibilities would be huge I made lame excuses to not meet with this person. I feared I would not be good enough and that It was all happening too fast. 554p

Tinna called. DJ messed up again. God hold my hand. I WILL WEATHER THIS. TURN PHONE OFF.

MARCH 24 7:34P
I weathered the storm. I was a bit scared but Joyce Myers book on "Hope" helped big time! I did turn my phone off however I turned it back on thinking I'm ok with anything that's texted to me and ok with the missed calls. Tinna texted me. Everything is ok. Smh.

Friday April 29 11:56pm
DJ here. He bought a piece of car with Momma (my mom) help of course. Him and Tinna finally turned in the rental car. My question is, if he here with the car that is supposed to be for both of them. How is she getting to work? She has no vehicle. She has been providing a ride for him since they been together! Now all of a sudden, he tired of her. He my son but he is the most selfish person I have ever met! I believe this is why everything he touch turns to shit. Plus he still using something. I'm gonna leave it be. I feel so bad for him. He cant live without using. No motivation, no ambition. Just talk. I gotta wait on the Lord. Please hurry Lord. In the meantime, I'm still in Toastmasters and its going well. I even have some possibilities in motivational speaking! Met with DEDE Perkins today at Starbucks. Imagine that. Me having a meeting at Starbucks! Unreal. Carrying my new briefcase. My first one got stolen out of the Z, along with the briefcase was the draft of the first speech I have no copies (long story).

I am so blessed. I must admit I am a little fearful of the unknown path I'm on right now, but I am going to do my best. Work hard and try to get out of my comfort zone. I met with DeDe concerning the "young lives" ministry. Has to do with helping and supporting teen moms. I need God to lead the way. Maybe my own ministry one day for young men! Lord please hold my hand. DJ making me kinda sad right now. My poor baby. Please Help Lord. Please 12:22p

　　　　　　　　　　GUILT, SHAME AND FEAR

DJ called so happy things worked out with the car...couple hours later he called back crying! God, please help him get off drugs and alcohol. Please!! 344p

The next few months were filled with the same 'ole ups and downs. It was like I was stuck in the world of DJ. Every time something happened with him, my hopes and dreams seemed less likely because I was being worn down by negativity. Smoking weed did not help. I had started smoking weed on a regular basis. Sometimes weed would relax me, and other times when I smoked, I would become anxious. It seemed like every time I smoked weed, DJ would call in distress. I'm serious . . . it was like clockwork. No more than an hour after I hit the weed, he would call, every time. I eventually took it as a sign to stop smoking. I decided to stop smoking weed while I was alone. I waited for hubby to come home. I stopped going to my Toastmasters International meetings, and eventually I stopped going to AA meetings too. I felt like I was a fraud because even though I had accomplished a few things, I was by all accounts, a weed head.

July 8, 2016 2:27p
Its been a while. A lot has happened.
1. *DJ and Tinna broke up*
2. *DJ depressed again*
3. *Car, car insurance in my name (hubby don't know)*
4. *He wont even try to buy things to keep the car running. just ridding around D.C.*
5. *Car breaks down, like I told the dummy it would if he didn't replace some of the small things that he could probably do himself. Take his mind off Tinna and give him something that he can call an accomplishment.*
6. *He got a new job, 90-day probation, missed 3 days already. Been suspended. One more strike and he's fired.*

He bought belts for the car weeks ago. Didn't put them on though. Belts pop. Now he needs to get to work. He asked me to pay his phone bill so he could call someone with tools to help him fix the car. I got so angry. I told him I was done. Don't call me. After I paid the bill. I told him if he was not my son, I would hate him I meant it when I said it but afterwards I was afraid that something else bad would happen because I said such an awful thing to my son. Its been two days and he hasn't called. I'm okay with that actually. I pray a lot these days. God has been good to me. People at work notice the change in me. I love God.

Ronney and I are in the process of buying our first home! Amazing. Stopped smoking weed for now. It started to give me negative thoughts. Not that I smoked much anyway. At first it used to help me relax enough to help me sleep, but it stopped working and negative thoughts, at times, is what I was left with. My mind tells me not to take weed to our new home. What do you think LORD? Hubby is okay with whatever decision is made.

Still in Toastmasters. This is not a cake walk but I'm doing fine I have given 4 of 10 speeches along with leadership roles. Started my book. I have written about 4000 words of the 15,000 words needed to complete a sixty-page book. Despite the pain I feel for my son I can honestly say I'm, okay with the life I have with my husband. Our Lord and savior Jesus Christ is always here. Till next time. 2:58pm

By now, I assume you get a clear picture of the mindset of a woman who was consumed by guilt. There were days that I felt I had overcome this condemnation of myself. There were days that I felt that God had my back. There were days when my son had normal days, and that was good for me mentally. Then there were days that I was gripped by fear. My friends, this is what is known as the transition from shame, guilt, and fear to spirituality. Remember, it is a process.

Let us fast forward a little to the year 2017.

GUILT, SHAME AND FEAR

August 22, 2017 2:22p

DJ has, for the past year or more, been getting worse. It makes me so sad inside. My baby is suffering. But he is also causing our family and anyone else associated with him a lot of grief. He upsets Momma and that makes me angry. He has been in some type of conflict or crisis, seemingly, every day. This breaks my heart. He got arrested last night for FIRST DEGREE ASSAULT! I have been praying so much for him to find some peace. Stop using. This is the most serious charge yet. I'm scared, hurt, sad and still somehow, I have to know that God , in His way, will stop the train that is my son. I hope he gets the help he needs. I feel fear and relief. Please Lord keep him safe. Amen 3:00pm

In this entry, I mentioned relief. I was relieved because my son was in jail for two reasons. First, he would be able to get the help he needed through the court system. The court system has saved a lot of men that I know personally because when you lose your freedom, sometimes it's a wakeup call, and the courts order offenders like myself to go to drug and alcohol programs to satisfy a sentence. A lot of the people end up in the rooms of Alcoholic Anonymous or Narcotics Anonymous. Secondly, I was relieved because the women in his life could breathe a sigh of relief at the prospect of peace.

AUGUST 30, 2017 11:53a

I've been doing a lot of crying. I've been doing a lot of smiling to keep from crying. Bills are piling up. My son still acting crazy, even while he sits in jail. I'm scared for DJ. I pray that God will be his Comforter and his Protector. I fainted Sunday because I became overtaken by fear, fear that I know is Satan. I joined church Sunday too. New Macedonia. The only thing that makes my life purposeful is the ability to do for my grandchildren. I'm broke but I will always find a way to get what they need. Today I decided to cry on my mothers' shoulder for the first time in my 51 years. I'm so thankful for her. I have been humbled. I no longer am able to portray myself as a strong, spiritually grounded woman. I no longer feel like I have my shit together. Praise God, for once I feel just like everyone else. For now, I feel free to be imperfect. My husband is my earthly rock. God is my spiritual rock, my salvation. Mom is gonna help me get my bills back on trac. She gave me the guidance that I've been longing for, but I just didn't realize it. I kept trying to figure out who to call, who can help me out of the pit I was falling into. Of all people, My mother! The one I had resented for so many years. She is my rock. I'm so happy to finally be able to have an emotional bond with her. This is such a blessing. Thank you, Father, 12:05p

SEPTEMBER 17, 2017 11:00p
We are going into the negative again (bank account). Ronney still not working as many hours as he used to, so bills are piling up. Its so stressful. DJ's court date is Tuesday. I am scared. Please Lord. Last week I felt alone. No one to cry to. It seems I have backed myself into a corner because I have to make everything appear to be ok. I feel like a hypocrite. All of this I have to feel without my vice, weed. I quit about two weeks ago. I wanted to go get some so bad. Boo said NO! My whole life being is consumed with the well-being of DJ. I don't know what I would do if he had to be away for a long time. I'm scared for my baby. Ke'shannah called last night. She misses her father. Broke my heart. I need to reach out to someone because I am beginning to isolate myself from the world. Reaching out for anyone, especially another woman is extremely difficult for me. I had fun playing cards and talking smack the other night but as the evening went on my mind went back to DJ. I feel like I had to keep those feelings to myself. Its hard. Oh yeah, I got bit by something 2 weeks ago and it looks bad. Still itching like hell. What's next!! Never mind, I really don't want to know the answer to that. My spirituality appears to be wavering. If I lose that I have nothing left. Please Father help my family. Please. I'm scared Lord 11:28

Tuesday Oct 10, 2017 941a
Its been over a month since my last entry. During that time what has happened is unbelievable. First, DJ ends up going to jail with the possibility of 25 years in prison. That possibility was almost debilitating for me.

I get anxious and scared when he does. I told him he has to man-up. And he did. He said "ma its gonna be okay" As soon as he said those words my eyes filled with tears.

As I write this part of the book, I remembered that as a child and throughout my addiction that those four words are what I wanted someone, anyone to say to me. To hear them first from my son was very moving. Ain't God good!

The last entry in my first journal was on Tuesday, June 26, 2018 at 7:38 p.m.

Between October 2017 and June 2018, life was still throwing me curve balls. My son still had a lot more suffering to do, and that was okay because as I sit here, I know for a fact that after the suffering is done, anything else would be a bump in the road. That's just the way life is. My son's life is his life. I had come to the point where I had to let go of everything that I felt I needed to hold on to as it relates to my son, and let God. The reality was that I needed to focus on my relationship with God in order to find and maintain peace of mind and spirit. Although we may go through seasons of suffering, no matter how long, we must take comfort in knowing that suffering sends us directly to our Lord and Savior, Jesus Christ.

We sometimes feel like the storm will never end and that we cannot make it through, but the real truth is that we always make it through our mental suffering. Just take a look back at all you have overcome so far. From the time my Uncle James molested me, to feeling unloved, to challenges in learning, to insecurities and resentments, to physical abuse and addiction, I was being groomed for a life full of amazing blessings!

Even though the things or persons that caused me to suffer still existed, I had changed. Today, I enjoy my life. Today, I am able to see beyond what is in front of me, for the most part. I know that everything in our lives happens for a reason.

The condemnation I suffered at my own hands and the fear I felt at the possibility of losing my child was over. Don't get it twisted, no one is ever fully prepared to lose a child, but we must not focus on that when we can focus on what is tangible and true, and that is God the Father. We have to find a way to let our children choose to live their lives in his or her own way and not ours. In the end, "It's gonna be okay."

My point in revealing my most inner thoughts and feelings through the words of my journal is to relate with those who have felt the same feelings I have felt. To hear that someone else has gone through the same mental challenges as I have makes this story more relatable. God revealed to me each time I was afraid that all will be well and guess what? It was.

It is now January 2021. My son is doing so much better. He is becoming the person that I always knew he would be, hardworking and thoughtful. He still has a ways to go, in my opinion, but the point is that Darryl is on his way to having the peace of mind and spirit that we all crave. When I see that my son is calling, my first thought is not *Oh Lord, what is going on now.* Instead, I prepare myself for a lengthy conversation about life. He has been humbled repeatedly. He realizes that God has been working in his life the whole time. Remember, look back and you will be so amazed!

I am not naïve to the fact that at any moment my son may have a mental relapse. We are all subject to this fate, but my position is from a mother's standpoint. I know that he has a better understanding about life, and he believes that Jesus is our Lord and Savior. What more can a mother wish for than a child who believes in God, not because I told him to, but through his own momentary relief from suffering. When we believe that God is in charge, there is a good chance that we can make it through anything. God does not keep us from suffering, but He walks us through it.

Many of us have suffered through abuse, beginning in our childhood. There will come a time when that abuse hampers us in one way or another, so we must tackle it head on. We must deal with the mess beneath the mess.

My son will have to tackle this task eventually. Until then, he has just scratched the surface of how much peace a spiritual life gives us but he has everything he needs to find peace. He believes in God, and he is beginning to believe in himself.

Saturday morning 2022… only three months into the new year and the suffering continues for my son. I increasingly feel a sense of dread. I still have faith in the power of God and I believe that God loves my son and will take care of him, however, I feel the need to prepare myself for the unimaginable, my son's death. I am torn, on one hand I believe that the things I put into the atmosphere sometimes come back to me and I don't want to speak about such a thought to anyone but on the other hand I want to brace myself for such an outcome. My comfort is that my son will finally have peace. The women and children who have suffered will have continuous peace. The perfect scenario would be that my son gets the help he needs to recover from the abuse, minimal nurturing and abandonment he suffered as a child and the addiction he battles as an adult.

There is an inner self that we hide from the world. We must get in touch with this "other self." I tend to embrace my other self—it is a place of safety. My son has an "other self" that exists in him. When we tackle the mess beneath the mess that is our past, we will find this "other self".

THE OTHER SELF

Deep within the soul of everyone,

There dwells a being different far from

The one that walks and talks and moves

With fellowman.

Deep within the makings of each mind,

There lie desires, emotions, never brought to light,

Never given out, expressed or shown

To fellowman

Deep within the heart of everyone,

Are corners which no mortal ever sees,

Where memories are added year by year

And over some we smile and some we grieve.

Deep within the mold of you and me,

Lies the other self, a being quite apart;

A being that is shy and real and true;

The only lasting part of me and you,

The other self, not shown to fellowman

MARIAN FOSTER SMITH

GUILT, SHAME AND FEAR

FEAR AND ANXIETY, THE LAST TO GO

FEAR IS A debilitating force. Fear will keep us from growing in every area of life. Fear keeps us from enjoying life to the fullest. There are all types of fear and, if you are anything like me, you have experienced most or all the following, not necessarily in this order:

1. Failure
2. Success
3. Social gatherings
4. Judgment
5. Loss
6. The unknown
7. Confrontation
8. Humiliation

Each fear was appointed to contrasting times of my life and one thing is certain, insecurity and low self-worth were often the catalyst of all the things that cause me to be fearful or anxious.

Unlike the memorized Toastmasters International speeches I had given, I cannot memorize what it is I need to say during an everyday conversation with someone. Sometimes when I speak to someone I begin to stumble over my words. I know what I want to convey, but depending on who I am speaking to, I would get anxious. I have noticed that sometimes the person I am speaking to has a puzzled look on their face as if to say, "What is she talking about?" It is embarrassing. I need to tell the whole story if not I will leave out key details and even then, I still tended to leave something out and not many of us have time to listen to the whole story.

During conversations my attention to the conversation gets a little shaky after about 45 seconds into the conversations. Any longer than that, I will miss key points of the conversation because my focus shifts for a second or two. In this case, I must think of something to say that I believe is relative to the conversation, sometimes I get it right, other times...not so much. No one has ever actually said "that doesn't have anything to do with what were talking about" but I can tell that they are a bit confused by my shift in the conversation. I feel foolish a lot of times because of this.

Now a days I have no problem asking questions after the conversation or during a conversation. I also jot down key words on a note pad as reminders of the questions I need to ask. I have also gotten good at working on several tasks at once because not much holds my attention for long; I have learned to use this aspect to my advantage, it works for me.

I am thoroughly convinced that I suffer from attention deficit hyperactivity disorder on some level. I have not been diagnosed by a doctor of any kind. I am not an expert on the topic either but as mentioned earlier in this book, I believe that I have educated myself just enough about attention deficit hyperactivity disorder to recognize the signs and symptoms of this disorder in myself.

In an October 14, 2021, a Healthline.com article, written by Erica

Roth and Kerry Weiss and medically reviewed by Marc S. Lener, MD explains that ADHD is a chronic condition that affects an individual's emotions, behavior and the ability to learn new things and this disorder mainly affects children, but can also occur in adults too.

The article goes on to describe the types of ADHD, there are three types:

- Inattentive type
- Hyperactive-impulsive type
- Combination type

Each one is tied to one or more characteristics: inattention and hyperactive-impulse behavior, says the authors of this article.

Inattention: getting distracted, having poor concentration and organizational skills.

Hyperactivity-never seeming to slow down, talking and fidgeting, difficulties staying on task.

Impulsivity-interrupting, taking risk.

Of course, the combined type is symptoms of both and not necessarily all the symptoms. Here is the kicker for me: one the speculated cause of ADHD is living in a chaotic environment.

As I have gotten older, I can manage most of my behaviors, I can even use them to my advantage but as a child, one could see how any of these behaviors would cause a child to withdraw just as I had.

Before I became comfortable with everything that makes me, me, I used to feel the need to escape when I was around other people. To be quite honest I still feel the need to get away from gatherings of more than three people in work environments but not so long ago, it could have been a family function, a gathering with old friends or those I was not familiar with, it didn't matter, I always felt that I was inferior to everyone else and that I would be judged or even ridiculed by someone in attendance. This is social anxiety, yet another catalyst of fear.

Along with social anxiety is also social phobia. There is a difference between the two.

I Google searched the difference in the two and came across an excerpt from a bridgestorecovery.com article, you gotta love Google! The excerpt says "Social phobia refers to the fears of being scrutinized and judged while performing some type of task in public, while social anxiety describes feelings of intense nervousness and self-consciousness that sufferers experience during one -on-one meetings or social gatherings".

The excerpt goes on to note that "social phobia develops out of excessive self-consciousness combined with lack of confidence and shaky self-esteem. People with social phobia are afraid to make a mistake while in the spotlight, fearing harsh and catastrophic judgements if they do so. The fear of embarrassment is off the charts and difficult to manage". "Social anxiety symptoms are often compared to the "fight or flight" response, where the body mobilizes rapidly to escape danger". The story of my life.

I am getting better at being around others because I have more confidence now than I have ever had at any time in my life, however the main reason I can cope much better is because of my connection to spirituality.

Those of us who suffer from fear of judgment tend to overcompensate. I was afraid that others would discover that I was uncomfortable, and they might judge me.

I always try harder to "shine" in all areas of our lives. I try to be better than anyone else at everything we do to compensate for what I believe are our flaws. I need to have the best of everything. There is nothing wrong about wanting the best, but my motives at the time were the issue. I call this dressing up the outside to compensate for what is really going on inside—insecurity.

I am okay with where I am in my life, and as far as being judged by others goes, I could care less, most times. I still feel the need to shine, but not for the same reasons as before—to satisfy what we feel others will judge us on. I want to shine as an example of what God can do!

Fear of the unknown could be the result of lack of preparation. If we go into any situation prepared, no matter what it is, our anxiety lessens. We may still have challenges, but at least we are able to begin this undertaking confidently. You may not believe this, but others recognize confidence in us, and when we display confidence, even if we are not, people will respect what we say, even if they do not agree with us. "Fake it till you make it," as the old saying goes.

Anxiety stems from fear. Anxiety and Fear are alert systems for our bodies. The two separate, in that, anxiety is concentrated in internal threats and fear is grounded in "known" external threats. Even if the threats are only perceptions, our minds and bodies react the same when it comes to fear and anxiety.

In earlier chapters fear was the term I used to describe some parts of my life. I can honestly say that anxiety had its way with me on many of those occasions. Fear definitely fit the case when I spoke of my son in the pages of my journal. Although the external threat of fear never came to fruition, the feelings I felt were fruitful enough. I lived almost twenty years seeing the external threats posed to addicts and alcoholics that are very real because we put ourselves in situations that are not conducive to safety. Not only that, but death is a real threat. For example, one evening while I was on one of my many missions of chasing crack, I picked up a guy I did not know. We started out driving around in my future husband's red sports car from place to place getting high; he had all the drugs. At around two or three a.m., we were sitting in the parked car, "geeking" trying to figure out where the next hit was coming from. Suddenly, this guy pulled out a knife, put the point of the knife on my side and said, "Take your clothes off." It was late; there were no lights on in the houses in this neighborhood. *What the heck was I going to do?* I thought. I knew that if this dude raped me, he could also stab me to death. I jumped out of the car as he tried to grab me. I screamed to the top of my lungs, "Fire, fire, fire!", I had learned from somewhere that screaming *fire* works better that screaming *help* because most people will not get involved for whatever reason, especially at that time of night but if you scream *fire* it is likely that a neighbor would be a lot more concerned, As I started to run I looked for a light to come on somewhere so I could get help but no one came outside nor did I notice anyone peaking from the windows, that I could see. As I ran, I looked back just long enough to notice that the man who had just pulled a knife on me had gotten out of the car and was running in the opposite direction. I hauled ass back to the red sports car, started the car and hurriedly pulled off. As I drove forward, peering in the rear-view mirror, a porch light from one of the houses on came on. This is just one of many nights where my life was threatened. Addicts and alcoholics tend to be oblivious to danger we put ourselves in as we leave the reality of the world behind for the sake of our substance of choice. God has always been with me, even in my darkest hours. And yes, fear is the appropriate term to use in that part of my story.

Everything we have discussed from the very beginning ends in fear and ultimately, anxiety.

I remember clearly and exactly how and when my spiritual self rose from beneath the weight of fear and anxiety. The rise started in Alcoholics Anonymous (AA) in 2012.

AA is where I came to believe there is, in fact, a power greater than myself. I had to give up the belief that I needed to oversee fixing all that was wrong with me, in my own way, and in my own time. Imagine how stressed I became trying to play God, Jr. The battle was His, and His alone. I learned that we are merely vessels in the work of our Lord and Savior. All I needed to do was look back over my life and I clearly saw all that I had survived. The revelation was quite overwhelming. I began to feel as if I was highly favored by God the Father.

Once spirituality was revealed as a real and tangible way to overcome the forces that life had bombarded me with from childhood to adulthood, I was able to finally see the light at the end of the tunnel. Alcoholics Anonymous forced me to look at how child molestation, lack of nurturing, and challenges with remaining focused were the catalysts that kept me drunk or high. In essence, I was covering up the pain of enduring emotional and mental trauma.

GUILT, SHAME AND FEAR

I began to speak at our meetings instead of just sitting in the room trying to poke holes in someone else's story. Soon after, my fellow "friends of Bill Wilson" began asking me to be the main speaker at some of our club's anniversary celebrations. The confidence I had in myself was on the rise at this point, despite the severe anxiety I still felt. Only God could do that!

I began doing the work of uncovering the mess beneath the mess. Every year after 2012, no matter what I was going through, whether it was self-pity, my son, guilt, shame, fear, or anxiety, the closer I got to God, the closer I got to freedom— spiritual freedom.

There are readings that occur before every AA meeting. One of the readings that took hold of me almost immediately was the Step Nine Promises:

> "If we are painstaking about this phase of our development, we will be amazed before we are halfway through. We are going to know a new freedom and a new happiness. We will not regret the past nor wish to shut the door on it. We will comprehend the word serenity and we will know peace. No matter how far down the scale we have gone, we will see how our experience can benefit others. That feeling of uselessness and self-pity will disappear. We will lose interest in selfish things and gain interest in our fellows. Self-seeking will slip away. Our whole attitude and outlook upon life will change. Fear of people and of economic insecurities will leave us. We will intuitively know how to handle situations which used to baffle us. We will suddenly realize that God is doing for us what we could not do for ourselves. *AA Big Book pages 83-84.*

Another pivotal moment for me was in 2016, the year I joined Toastmasters International. God began to direct me on a path that would have me come face-to-face with my worst fears—judgment, humiliation, and social interactions. I was thrown into the arena with people who I believed, at the time, were more successful and more educated than me.

It was the first speech I had written and given to this room full of people from different backgrounds, different countries, and different races, men and women. The first speech I gave was a "screaming out" of what "they had done to me," so to speak. A speech about being molested by my uncle, a speech about feeling unloved, which ended with Psalms 91. A co-worker sent me this scripture and ever since that day, I have been able to find comfort in the words of this psalm. It felt to me as if God were speaking directly to me. I felt safe from all that I feared whenever I reflected on this psalm. Read it, and you will know exactly what I am talking about.

Here is Psalms 91 from the New International Version of the Bible:

"Whoever dwells in the shelter of the Most High
will rest in the shadow of the Almighty.

I will say of the Lord, "He is my refuge and my fortress, my God, in whom I trust." He will cover you with his feathers, and under his wings you will find refuge; his faithfulness will be your shield and rampart.

You will not fear the terror of night,
nor the arrow that flies by day,
nor the pestilence that stalks in the darkness,
nor the plague that destroys at midday.
A thousand may fall at your side,
ten thousand at your right hand,
but it will not come near you.
You will only observe with your eyes
and see the punishment of the wicked.
If you say, "The Lord is my refuge,"
and you make the Most High your dwelling,
no harm will overtake you,
no disaster will come near your tent.

GUILT, SHAME AND FEAR

For he will command his angels concerning you
to guard you in all your ways, they will lift you up in their
hands, so that you will not strike your foot against a stone. You
will tread on the lion and the cobra;
you will trample the great lion and the serpent.
"Because he loves me," says the Lord, "I will rescue him; I will
protect him, for he acknowledges my name.
He will call on me, and I will answer him.
I will be with him in trouble,
I will deliver him and honor him.
With long life I will satisfy him
and show him my salvation."
Psalm 91

When we have challenges of any kind as children, we are ill-prepared to handle them without help from the adults in the room and if, as in my case, the adults in the room are part of the problem, where do we turn?

Shame, guilt, and fear turned out to be the catalysts of spirituality for me. As I mentioned previously, not all my life was permeated with these particular catalysts, but the aftermath of such things left me with a lifelong battle with anxiety.

I really do hope that at the very least, one person who reads this book and has gone through their own bout with shame, guilt, and fear, will find comfort and understanding, and courage to overcome all that ails you spiritually.

Philippians 4:6-8 (NJKV) tells us to "be anxious for nothing, but in everything by prayer and supplication [humbly ask], with thanksgiving, let your request be made known to God and the peace of God, which surpasses all understanding, will guard your hearts and minds through Jesus Christ."

Amen

THE PRODUCT OF THE CATALYSTS—SPIRITUALITY

SPIRITUALITY SEEMED FARFETCHED to me in the beginning. It is not an easy task to go from the storms of life to the safe harbor of trusting in God. We try to hold on to our way of doing things for as long as humanly possible because we think we are in control of what happens to us, good or bad. To a degree, we may have some control, but here is the problem with that—we use the same mind that created the storms to fix the storms.

Our minds, souls, and spirits must begin to align before spirituality or trust in God start to take root in our lives. I believe that if it were not for shame, guilt, and fear, I would not have found myself on a mission of relief—a mission to spirituality. We must go through the fire before the flames of inner turmoil, also called suffering, subside. Spiritual growth is an ongoing endeavor. Life will always present us with ample opportunity to do just that—grow.

When we are amid a growing season through spiritual wounds and spiritual bankruptcies, we often withdraw from our responsibilities. I would turn off my phone so I would not be disturbed by negativity. I would take mental days from work too, just to stay on the right track because spiritual growth took a lot of effort for me. I figured that if I just removed myself from the trouble life was sure to bring, I would be able to grow spiritually. It does not work that way. We must be able to live life, whatever the struggles may be, as best we can in a spiritual manner. Remember, if not for the struggles, spirituality does not exist, at least not early on. After a while, we begin to understand that it is how we respond to our struggles that measure our spiritual growth.

Early on in my growing season, I could not live life on life's terms and practice spirituality at the same time. Meaning, I would get so frustrated by what was going on in my life that I would just say, "Eff it," and revert to the old me.

There will come a time in your journey when you say to yourself, "I am tired of being the bigger person," "I am tired of doing the right thing and having to be polite about it," "I am tired of putting others first while they act selfishly."

When I get "tired," it lets me know that I should be doing less talking about spirituality and more walking in spirituality. The choices or actions we make during our, almost certain, bouts of spiritual wounds and bankruptcies are a clear sign of our progress or lack thereof. But what is exponentially more indicative of our progress, is the way we feel in a particular situation. Here is the deal—long after our frustration and angry actions have been displayed, the feelings of another failed attempt at being our new selves lingers, prompting us to surrender, yet again. Remember, the process of spiritual growth repeats itself. Wounds, bankruptcies, growth. Wounds, bankruptcies, and growth. Continuous surrendering is all part of the ongoing process.

In the beginning of our spiritual journeys, spirituality is short lived, but the more we practice trusting and having faith that God will do for us what we cannot do for ourselves, the better our lives become. I tell people all the time, "It's good on this side." No matter how brief our spiritual experiences are, the benefits that arise from the process are priceless. Just wait and see!

I am not a professional in this matter.

I am not a religious person.

I am flawed.

I am another you.

I have no formal education as it relates to psychology nor am I an authority on spirituality. I come to you with years of enduring emotional and mental challenges that have given me hands-on and real-life experiences in the area of spirituality.

Education and real-life experiences are included in how we overcome our most challenging situations. In my case, I was actively overcoming the remnants of emotional trauma. I am not saying enroll in college or any online classes. I am suggesting that you read a book or two about what you believe is going on with you to get a better understanding of what you are dealing with. You don't have to read a book as thick as the Bible on the altar at church. Reading *Battlefield of the Mind* by Joyce Myer was pivotal in the beginning of my journey because her book enlightened me about pain, forgiveness, and how the Devil works to keep us in bondage. Once I started reading about my challenges and realizing that I was not alone in this battle of the mind, I was able to understand the feelings that were raging inside me.

Let us delve into what the formal experts have to say about spirituality. First, what is spirituality?

Spirituality means different things to different people. For me, spirituality is the existence of peace of mind and spirit.

According to Mastin Kipp, the author of *Daily Love: Growing in Grace*, spirituality is the measure of how willing we are to allow Grace—some power greater than ourselves—to enter our lives and guide us along the way.

Wikipedia defines spirituality this way, "According to Kees Waaijman, the traditional meaning of spirituality is the process of reformation which 'aims to recover the original shape of man, the image of God.'"[1] To accomplish this, the re-formation is oriented at a mold, which presents the original shape; In Judaism the Torah, in Christianity there is Christ, for Buddhism, Buddha, and in Islam, Muhammad.

According to an "Explore God" article by Tim Keller, spiritual growth is exhibited in what is called the fruit of the spirit. In Galatians 5:22-23, the fruit of the spirit is listed as love, joy, peace, forbearance, kindness, goodness, faithfulness, gentleness, and self-control.

In the online article, "Spirituality - What does it really mean?" by Alfred James for Pocket Mindfulness, he explains that "Spirituality is an internal sanuary, free of rules and expectations of the spiritual world, it is a place where one can submit to ones mortality and rest properly, without worry, anxiety, desire and striving". Alfred James goes on to say, "In the arms of Spirituality, one is comforted by an understanding of the transient (fleeting) nature of life, that no matter who we are or where we come from, we are all a part of the same cycle of life."

I have nothing against the teachings of any deity like Allah, Buddha, etc. because they all offer the same thing, spirituality. A belief in something higher than ourselves that inspires us to be better people. I chose Christianity because it is the practice I grew up with and have become a part of over the years.

In the beginning of my spiritual journey, I did not actually believe or have much faith in a power greater than yours truly. My belief at the time was that if I broke it, whatever it was, I alone had to fix it, and I alone would take the credit for the outcome. I prayed the prayer we all have prayed at least once in our lifetime, "Lord, if you get me out of this, I will never do it again." This prayer of desperation was the beginning of my relationship with spirituality. I prayed this prayer many times during my cocaine addiction. I am speaking of the times in the wee hours of the morning when I was sitting in somebody's crack house, again. I was unsure where my next hit would come from, how I was going to get home, what I would tell my man whenever I did get home. I remember the sick feeling I had in my gut, I was sick

1

of being "like this," however, spirituality did not cross my mind, but I knew enough to pray to God. God heard every insincere prayer, I made it home every single time, but I was still sick. It was as if the moment I exited the crack house was the moment the conversation ended between me and God.

For a long while, spirituality meant that I had to be perfect, I could not live up to this high bar. I was either too fearful or too apprehensive about being spiritual to claim that I was, and not feel like a fraud. This thought process led me to the ignorant conclusion that I was the sole force behind the new life I had made for myself, without help from anyone or anything.

Attending AA meetings on a regular basis was the higher power for me at the time. I spoke a lot about how to get to a point in my sobriety that I was as happy and spiritually grounded as the other members appeared to be. My one-year anniversary was approaching, but I did not feel happy, joyous and free nor did I feel spiritual about my one-year anniversary because I had been clean for eight years prior to coming to the rooms of Alcoholics Anonymous in 2012, so one year did not excite me one bit. All I knew was that something was missing from my soul, a relationship with my Higher Power, spirituality. My soul was still in turmoil even though I had not drank or drugged in a year. I wanted peace in every area of my life.

I spoke to my sponsor about how I felt, and she suggested that I go to an AA meeting somewhere other than the meeting I had been attending up to this point. I did.

The topic of the hour would be Step two of AA's twelve steps to sobriety, "We came to believe that a power greater than ourselves could restore us to sanity." Coincidence, I think not.

One member used as an analogy, an evidence bag. This bag was filled with evidence that God is real and has been working on his behalf all along.

I thought to myself, "evidence bag." He told us what was in his imaginary bag of evidence. I do not remember any of what he may

GUILT, SHAME AND FEAR

have mentioned because I was deep in my own thoughts, I had drifted away from the meeting. I began to fill up my bag of evidence with all that God had brought me through.

One day, while I was out on another mission, I ended up inside an apartment with a guy who I had hooked up with. I don't remember how we hooked up, but I knew that he was interested in me. I felt nothing for him, just like I felt nothing for any of the other hookups I met, I just wanted to get high, and that is what I intended to do at any cost.

We were sitting at the dining room table getting high when I had to go to the bathroom. As soon as I went in and shut the door, this guy came in and just grabbed me, he was trying to tear my clothes off. I fought so hard. I yelled for someone to come in and help me. There were at least three other people in the apartment, but not one crackhead came to rescue me. I can't say that I was scared because this guy was almost as small as me, but it was clear that he was stronger than me, especially since he was high on crack. I managed to get out of the bathroom. That was God.

Side note: I did not leave the apartment after that, believe it or not. I went back to the dining room table and smoked crack from the guy that five minutes ago tried to rape me. I also returned the next day telling this guy I had Aids so he would leave me alone, guess what? He said he had Aids too.

I had a guy pull a knife on me in an attempt to rape me, I had a guy put a gun to my head.

One night, or early morning, I am not sure of the exact time, but I was usually walking alone when it was dark outside because I did not want to be seen by anyone. One night, I was walking through the woods, yes, the woods, it was a short cut. I had a habit of walking with my head down, as I got further into the path, I raised my head and I spotted what looked like a man sitting on a fallen tree. It was too late to turn back. By the time I saw him I was about three feet away from him. He did not say a word. I think I said hi or something. Anyway, I made my way past him without incident. All I could remember thinking was where did he come from? Why was he just sitting there on the fallen tree at this time of morning? I looked back once I got out of the woods, he was gone. Gods' hands were all over that incident. God has been protecting me for as long as I can remember.

There are a multitude of other pieces of evidence I added to my bag that day. That AA meeting made me excited about my first anniversary and about spirituality.

A relationship begins with a conversation and is maintained the same way, along with other spiritual practices, like giving and reading the Word to learn more about the power of a higher power. Spirituality is the essence of a relationship with your Higher Power. There is no greater gift from the Lord than peace. Peace is what I have chased ever since the first time I felt it while sitting alone in the sanctuary of a church. That, my friends, was the peace that surpassed all understanding.

In the beginning of a spiritual journey, spirituality is short-lived, but the more you practice it, the better it gets. No matter how brief your spiritual experiences are, the benefits that arise from this process are priceless.

Spirituality is being blessed with riches for which there is no comparison. Spirituality cannot be brought or sold. However, there is a price to pay for this magnificent connection to God and the Holy Spirit, and that is through suffering of some kind. My friends, we all need to have some measure of spirituality. Once we are blessed with even a miniscule part of it, we should take every opportunity to enhance or deepen it. It's so much better on this side y'all.

HIS KIND OF LOVE

HIS KIND OF love is like the morning sun in its brilliant yellow glow, its warmness caressing your face, the intoxicating scent of lavender flowers, just feet away. The feeling of His familiar embrace guiding you to rest in the soft blanket that is his vest. He whispers" it is okay my child" you are safe. I am here.

His kind of love assures you; your loved one is warm and safely tucked away from any harm. He assures you that laughter and peace will prevail in the days coming. He assures you that your mind and body will be rejuvenated to its natural place. He says" I will cover you both beneath my wings". "The morning will become joyful again. I promise"

His kind of love is the feeling you get when you have given all you have, but His grace and mercy still seem to allude you; you feel unworthy and unloved, your faith has dwindled to nothing. Purposefully, His kind of love directs you to a place, a place that is quiet and beautiful. The water today somehow seems quite blue. The old dead tree you saw before has buds on it. The grass is freshly manicured, its aroma so nice, people off in the distance, relaxing, soft jazz playing. You wonder "Why am I here?" He says" I know every hair on your head, you are my beloved child. This place supplies the peace you need to hear Me again, My undivided attention belongs to you because you are worthy and My promises to you will come to pass at the right time. I instilled this place in your heart today, go now and know that I am with you through suffering, no harm to you will succeed. I will never leave you".

"This kind of love" leads us to "His kind of love", forever.

Pamela M. Walker
Copyright©2022

CPSIA information can be obtained
at www.ICGtesting.com
Printed in the USA
LVHW081204210223
739960LV00017B/1604